THE FOREST FOR THE TREES

AN INTRODUCTION TO SOCIOLOGICAL THINKING

THE FOREST FOR THE TREES

AN INTRODUCTION TO SOCIOLOGICAL THINKING

ALLAN G. JOHNSON

UNDER THE GENERAL EDITORSHIP OF
ROBERT K. MERTON
COLUMBIA UNIVERSITY

Harcourt Brace Jovanovich College Publishers
Fort Worth   Philadelphia   San Diego
New York   Orlando   Austin   San Antonio
Toronto   Montreal   London   Sydney   Tokyo

ISBN: 0-15-527903-3

Library of Congress Catalog Card Number: 90-83667

Printed in the United States of America

PREFACE

——— ◆ ———

On the most practical level, I wrote this book to provide a concise, critical introduction to the main conceptual and theoretical frameworks that make sociological thinking a distinctive approach to understanding the world. My deeper purpose, however, is based on the belief that we will not make substantial progress toward improving the human condition without developing and applying a collective ability to think about and understand social systems — how they operate, the consequences they produce, and the different ways in which we as individuals can choose to participate in them.

In this sense, *The Forest for the Trees* is not simply a description of what sociology is about; it is a deeply felt argument promoting sociological thinking as a way of approaching human life and as an alternative to the psychological individualism that so dominates thinking today, especially in the United States. It is my hope that readers will acquire not only some understanding of what it takes to think sociologically, but also a clearer sense of why the development of this ability is worth the effort.

As we go to press, I am mindful of those who have helped to transform this work into a finished book. I thank Robert K. Merton who, as Harcourt Brace Jovanovich's general editor in sociology, has once again offered up his generous supply of support and useful criticism; my editor David Watt, whose fine critical abilities and ear for smooth-flowing prose are in evidence on every page; Marcus Boggs and Rick Roehrich, who eagerly supported the idea for this book from the start; Linda Sands for her elegant design; and production manager David Hough, whose responsibility it has been to guide the book into print. And to Nora Jamieson, whose support for my life and work helps make each book I write part of a life whose richness I would trade for none other, go my abiding respect, love, and deepest appreciation.

Allan G. Johnson

TABLE OF CONTENTS

— ◆ —

— ♦ —

The Forest
for the Trees

— ♦ —

Social Facts
and Social Life

The second half of the twentieth century in the United States has seen a virtual explosion in the popularity of individualism. The American creed of individualism, with its roots in the pioneering work of nineteenth-century psychologist William James and a revolutionary awareness of the subconscious that grew from the insights of Sigmund Freud, has deepened and broadened into a preoccupation with the individual life as the primary, if not only, framework for understanding the complexities and mysteries of human existence.

The best-seller lists overflow with titles promising new levels of self-awareness and self-improvement; in public discussion the workings of major institutions, from educational to international politics, are reduced to the personalities and behaviors of those who lead them; and the spiritual and psychological liberation of human consciousness is widely perceived as a New Age solution to social problems. The problems of poverty have been reduced to the habits and skills of the individual poor; war to aggressive impulses; drug abuse to the failure of individual will and good sense; extremes of inequality to individual poverty among nations to failures of leadership, talent, and will; and the ingrained prejudice and discrimination of sexism and racism to inadequate socialization resulting in personal ignorance and bad habits.

In short, we have embraced the idea that the key to understanding the organization of collective life lies in the internal and external manifestations of the individual life. Psychotherapy is increasingly identified not only as a means for enabling individuals to better understand themselves and chart new courses for their lives, but as a model for change at the social level as well. It is—to turn Karl Marx on his head—individual and not class consciousness that is widely perceived as the primary engine of positive social change. The solution to collective problems is perceived to lie not in collective solutions, but in the accumulation of individual solutions.

This view has been made possible by our increasing ability to be reflexive at the individual level, examining ourselves in order to be more aware, and think about and see ourselves in new ways. Our preoccupation is based on the growing importance of the *idea* of the individual as an entity that can somehow exist and be thought of apart from its social environment. Indeed, we have almost supplanted the idea of the social environment with the concept of the individual, as if groups and societies and even international systems are little more than a collection of individual psyches which, if understood psychologically, constitute all that we need to know about social life.

As appealing as this view is in the highly individualistic context of societies such as the United States, it fails to incorporate the crucial fact that the whole is more than the sum of its parts. The whole is, to be sure, constituted of its parts, but it is more than that, and it is the whole that we tend to ignore in our fixation on the parts. In short, we miss the forest for the trees.

Unfortunately, for many people the idea that the whole is more than the sum of its parts is obvious when made in reference to just about everything but human groups and societies; they resist the idea that there is anything about collections of people that cannot be reduced to and understood solely on the level of individuals. After all, since individuals participate in relationships, if we understand each person, don't we then know all we need to know about relationships?

While William James and Sigmund Freud were laying the groundwork for the psychological dimensions of American individualism, European and, to a lesser degree, U.S. sociologists were trying to develop a different kind of reflexivity that would enable us to understand the *collective* nature of social life that cannot be reduced to its manifestations in the lives of individuals. At the core of this view is the concept of a social system—a set of relationships that can be thought of as a whole. A family, for example, is a set of relationships among kin, just as a soccer team is a set of relationships among various player positions, and a world economy is a set of relationships joining, among other entities, nations and corporations. Although they vary enormously in their size and complexity, each of these—family, team, and world system—is a social system.

Émile Durkheim proposed that social systems cannot be fully understood without looking at them as entities in and of themselves whose characteristics and dynamics are not a simple accumulation of the characteristics and behaviors of individual people. Consider the phenomenon of suicide, for example, which occupied much of Durkheim's attention, resulting in his classic study that was probably the first to use systematic data in pursuit of sociological questions.[1] On the one hand, suicide is undeniably a highly individualistic act in which people knowingly bring about their own deaths. If we ask why people kill themselves we would discover answers including feelings of depression, worthlessness, hopelessness, loneliness, and guilt, as well as factors such as altruism or duty that lead some to forfeit their lives to benefit others.[2]

A suicide *rate*, on the other hand, cannot be explained in the same way as an individual suicide. If the suicide rate for the United States increased by fifty percent over a short period of time—from 12 suicides per 100,000 people to 18 per 100,000—what would we conclude? With an individualistic perspective, we might simply

---

[1] Émile Durkheim, *Suicide* (New York: The Free Press, 1951, Original edition, 1897).
[2] For a detailed summary of what is known about such factors, see David Lester, *Why People Kill Themselves* (Springfield, IL: Charles C. Thomas, 1983).

"sum" individual explanations to arrive at a "collective" explanation, which is to say that the rate of suicide increased because of increases in the psychological factors that prompt individuals to kill themselves—in feelings of depression, despair, worthlessness, and so on. Or, in finding that the suicide rate is much lower in one group than another, we might attribute it to differences in the prevalence and intensity of suicide-prone psychological states.

On the face of it, there is nothing wrong with such reasoning except that it tells us nothing about *why* feelings such as depression increase in a society or why they are more common in one group than another or why people in one social category are more likely to respond to such feelings in a suicidal way (rather than, for example, reaching out to others for emotional support or entering psychotherapy). Individual explanations cannot answer such questions because they do not apply to groups and societies. To understand individuals, it may be sufficient to focus on their characteristics, but to understand social systems as well as their effects on people, it is necessary to focus on the characteristics of those systems which are usually quite different from those of individuals. Unlike people, societies cannot be depressed or lonely; but they can include social arrangements that foster such feelings in people to varying degrees and they can encourage different ways of responding to them.

Rates are characteristics that describe social systems, not individuals. The fact that the suicide rate in the United States is roughly 12 suicides per 100,000 people tells us nothing about individuals: in any given year, each of us either commits suicide or we do not, and that cannot be determined from the rate. What the rate does indicate is something about the social environment in which populations of individuals live. When the rate differs substantially from one social system to another, then we know that something about the characteristics of those systems to varying degrees promotes or discourages suicide as an individual behavior. This does not mean that what we know about the psychological causes of suicide is invalid or useless in understanding suicide as a phenomenon, only that it cannot fully explain different *patterns* of suicide that vary from one period or social system to another.

This holds true for the enormous range of indicators such as rates, percentages, and averages that describe aspects of human life at the collective level—from crime, birth, death, morbidity, marriage, divorce, and economic productivity rates, to the percentages of a population who vote, attend college, are wealthy or poor, work outside the home, believe in God, harbor racial prejudice, are victims of crime, attend baseball games, or support abortion rights, to averages for educational attainment, income, age at first marriage, number of children, weeks unemployed, or church attendance. In all of these cases the indicators would not exist were it not for the experiences and behaviors of individuals; however, the patterns they describe tell us not about those individual lives but the social contexts in which they are lived. Therefore, the explanation of such patterns must include the characteristics of those contexts.

"The whole is more than the sum of its parts" is an idea that manifests itself in many ways. In the most direct sense, it means that collective phenomena cannot be reduced to the simple sum of individual phenomena. To argue otherwise is like saying that all we need to know in order to understand a symphony is the frequency response of all the individual notes, how long and how loudly each is sounded, and which instruments play them. If we took all of the notes from Beethoven's Ninth Symphony and spread them out on the floor, how many years of searching through that pile would it take to identify it as Beethoven's Ninth? The sociological answer is that the question is a false one because the "it"—the pile of notes—is no more Beethoven's Ninth Symphony than it is anything else; it is the arrangement of the notes in relation to one another that makes the symphony, and the arrangement cannot be derived from the notes, singly or as a collection.

On one level, of course, a symphony must have notes just as social systems could not exist without people, but the sociological point is that symphonies and societies are more than that, just as human beings are more than a bunch of carbon-related molecules and water (although on one level we certainly are that). It is the "more than that" that sociology in general is concerned with. In a sense, most disciplines are concerned with one or another perspective on "more than that," which is to say, with the rich elaborations that we find when we go beyond the (thus far) irreducible levels of atomic and subatomic physics. Were it not for the fundamental fact that every whole is more than the sum of its parts—whether it be a human being, a society, or a rock—it is unlikely that there would be much to hold our attention for very long. Life would then appear to us as programs "appear" to computers, to whom software is indeed no more than a linear sum of parts. It is form and structure, in short, and the infinite variety that springs from them that make social life interesting. (While computers can certainly understand a program in a linear sense, I doubt that they will ever be able to appreciate the beauty of a program as a whole).

Social life cannot be fully understood simply by knowing about individuals without attention to the relationships that connect them to one another. If we observe a group of people hitting, injuring, and killing one another, we cannot simply conclude that they are engaging in what we know as warfare. War is not only aggressive behavior involving relatively large numbers of people—in fact, in tribal warfare it can involve a quite small number of people. It is neither the number nor the behavior that constitutes warfare; it is the social organization of the participants that differentiates random violence, riots, brawls, mobs, and warfare. In warfare, the society and not the individual combatant is the primary focus—the aggression is carried out in what are perceived to be the interests of the society as a whole, and individual participation is based upon identification with the society as well as (although not necessarily) with those interests.

If we ask individual soldiers to explain their participation in a war and then combine those responses, the result would most likely bear little resemblance to the social forces—the social conditions, government policies, goals, decisions, and so on—that actually caused the war. Soldiers generally do not fight for the grand ideological causes and national interests that prompt states to mobilize armies and declare wars. They are more likely to fight from a sense of duty to their countries or fear of appearing cowardly or unpatriotic to their neighbors, friends, and families; and once in combat, are motivated primarily to save their own lives and those of their comrades. Studies of the German army's performance during the final months of World War II, for example, found that the astonishing ability of small units to continue fighting under the most arduous conditions was due not to a deep belief in Nazi ideology or Germany but to the primary ties of affection and loyalty that bound individual soldiers to one another. Studies of American soldiers in Vietnam show similar results.[3]

---

[3]See E.A. Shils and M. Janowitz, "Cohesion and Disintegration in the Wehrmacht in World War II," *Public Opinion Quarterly* 12 (Summer 1948):280–315; M. Van Creveld, *Fighting Power: German and U.S. Army Performance, 1939–1945* (Westport, CT: Greenwood Press, 1981); and C.C. Moskos, "Why Men Fight: American Combat Soldiers in Vietnam," *Transaction* 7(1), 1969.

What identifies warfare as a social activity is not simply what people do or why they do it, but the social forces that bring them together and organize their behavior as enemies or allies. The same is true of all of the behaviors that constitute social life. If we think of a bureaucracy as simply a collection of people who behave in a bureaucratic way—who are obsessed with obeying the rules, who shuffle great quantities of paper, who continually worry about the person they are accountable to, who seem to care more about the rules and the organization than they do about people—we have it backwards, for it is bureaucracy as a social *arrangement* of people in particular kinds of hierarchical relations to one another that produces bureaucratic behavior, not the other way around. Bureaucracies—and families and sports teams and most other social systems—do not simply form spontaneously from the behavior of individuals; it is the behavior of individuals, rather, that is shaped and conditioned by bureaucratic social systems.

It is of course true, as some sociologists argue, that without people behaving in bureaucratically appropriate ways, there would be no bureaucracies, and in this sense social interaction is absolutely necessary to manifest a particular social arrangement.[4] But the crucial point here is that a bureaucracy is not simply a type of behavior, since all of the specific behaviors found among bureaucrats can be found in other social situations as well. A bureaucracy is, rather, a set of relationships through which such behavior is organized and from which it emerges and takes shape. Without participants sharing the perception and the assumption that such an arrangement in fact exists, they would have no reason to behave in such characteristic and predictable ways.

Another distinction between wholes and parts lies in the observation that individual and collective interests are often quite different from one another. A mainstay of capitalist ideology, for example, is the belief that in a free market the unrestrained pursuit of self-interest by individuals will have outcomes that also serve the best interests of communities and societies as a whole.[5] Individual profit is maximized when goods are bought or produced

---

[4] This is particularly true of the work of the symbolic interactionist Herbert Blumer, whose ideas are more fully discussed in Chapter 5.

[5] For a critique of this, see Barry Barnes, *About Science* (Oxford and New York: Basil Blackwell, 1985), Chapter 5.

for a low price and sold for a high one. In the case of real estate this means that in a profitable market prices will steadily escalate with each new round of buying and selling. As many affluent communities in Connecticut and elsewhere have found, this does maximize the gain of each individual property owner; but on a collective level it can have disastrous consequences. In many cases, housing prices have increased so rapidly that people who are vital to the town's welfare—police officers, administrators, school teachers, fire fighters, maintenance workers, health workers, and so on—cannot afford to live there, which threatens even the most affluent towns' ability to provide basic services. This collective outcome cannot be derived from each individual outcome or their simple "sum." It can only be foreseen and understood if we take into account how communities are organized as social systems.

If the whole—whether a symphony, a chair, or a social system—is more than the sum of its parts, then we can think of it as being in some sense separate from and external to the parts that comprise it. Just as physical environments exert pressures and limitations on us (through temperature, terrain, the pull of gravity, etc.), so, too, the characteristics of social environments affect us in ways that are in some respects external to us even though it is only through our participation in them that they exist. And just as the characteristics of physical environments constitute the physical facts of life, so, too, the characteristics of social systems constitute what Durkheim called social facts.[6]

Social facts are "social" in two basic ways: they constrain the way people think, feel, appear, and behave; and they derive their authority from being generally perceived as being collective and external to the individual lives in which their effects are manifested. Consider language, for example, which is a fundamental part of every social system. A language consists of a set of symbols (words, numbers, mathematical notation, or musical notes and notation) and rules (grammar and syntax) that govern how the symbols are arranged to create different meanings. Language constrains and limits us because we are generally confined to its set of symbolic categories for constructing representations of what we think, feel, perceive, and do. If there is no word for something, for example, we are less likely to notice it as significant. In this sense,

---

[6]Émile Durkheim, *The Rules of the Sociological Method* (New York: The Free Press, 1964. Original edition, 1895). See especially Chapter 1.

learning the names of things is an indispensable part of learning to focus attention on the world in a systematic and intentional way. As children acquire language, they literally narrow their world from the wide open, unfocused world of infant perceptions to the far more selective and cognitively and emotionally circumscribed world of adults.

Language both limits and empowers us. It empowers us by enabling us to construct representations of experience in symbolic terms and thereby think about, store, retrieve, and share them with others. It limits us by shaping the way in which those representations are made, confining us to a limited set of symbols. English, for example, is a particularly rich language because it includes many words that reflect more subtle shades of meaning than those found in most other languages. Two psychotherapists who conducted training workshops in Germany found that the German therapists they worked with preferred to do pyschother-apeutic work in English because it allows them greater flexibility and power in describing their emotions. The Germans have even found that as their knowledge of both English and therapy increases, dreams with special emotional significance are more likely to occur in English.[7]

What makes language a social fact is that we generally see it as something whose ultimate authority rests outside of us as individuals and, by extension, to some degree outside of us as a collection of individuals. The rules of grammar are regarded as correct and therefore to some degree binding on us not because we say they are correct or because everyone agrees they are correct. Indeed, we have no way of knowing how most people in our society actually regard the rules of grammar. The constraining power of language lies rather in the weight of our *assumption* that it is part of our social environment and therefore relatively immune from the desires of individuals or collections of individuals to challenge or alter its meanings and rules of usage arbitrarily. In speech and writing we can violate those rules or misuse words all the time, but this is very different from claiming that the dictionary meanings of words or the rules of grammar and syntax are themselves false and should be changed or discarded. It is difficult to imagine an individual or group of individuals believing they had the authority to argue that

---

[7] Stuart Alpert and Naomi Bressette of the Hartford Family Institute, Hartford, CT, personal communication.

"book" is the word for what we otherwise know to be a "banana" or that "bananas eats he yellow" is or should be an acceptable way of communicating that "He eats yellow bananas." This is because we regard language as part of our social environment, not part of individuals or groups of individuals.

It is of course true that language is not completely external to us or that we are powerless to change it. New words are added to our vocabulary at a sometimes astonishing rate and meanings of existing words change in response to how people actually use them. Language, like other aspects of social environments, is a dynamic phenomenon that shapes the lives of people and is, in turn, shaped by them. In this sense, to describe language as a social fact is not to say that language is nothing more than that; but it does say that every language is viewed to some degree as constraining and external to us, and this gives it social authority and importance. Language does not have authority as a part of culture because everyone actually uses it in a particular way; indeed, actual usage most likely violates the rules of language more often than not. The truth is the other way around: we assume that everyone will use language in a particular way because we assume it has authority as part of our culture, and it is this shared assumption that lies at the heart of social facts.

The same can be said of all kinds of cultural ideas, such as beliefs and values: we do not experience them as part of our social environment because most people actually support them; we think most people support them because we identify such ideas as part of our culture. What we identify as good and evil have an authority that transcends what we may actually think or believe at any given moment. When the "hero" stands up for a principle abandoned by a community in a frenzy of homicidal panic—such as happens with lynch mobs—and manages to carry the day, it is not the hero's personal authority that has the power to sway others so much as the appeal to an authority that goes beyond mere numbers, to a shared sense of "we" that is more than the sum of individuals and what they believe or want at the time.

Although Durkheim first introduced the concept of social facts a century ago, thinking about social systems as something more than a collection of individuals has developed very little outside of academic sociology. It is true that some of the terminology developed through sociological thinking—such as altruism, folkways, ethnocentrism, in-group, out-group, stereotype, white-collar crime, minority group, anomie, role, significant other, and self-fulfilling prophecy—has been incorporated into everyday usage, but although we may think in sociological *terms*, this is a far cry from thinking sociologically.[8] In the twentieth century, sociological thinking has not generated the kind of collective reflexivity that would realize its enormous potential to expand human understanding and empower communities and societies to shape the terms of social life in better ways.

Especially in the United States since World War II, sociologists have gathered great quantities of data bearing on a staggering array of social phenomena and issues, and in cases such as the documentation of poverty, the effects of racial segregation, or the efficacy of capital punishment, these findings have had some effect on social policy. But this generally has not been accompanied by a corresponding increase in awareness of and literacy in thinking about social systems *as* systems. As will be shown in Chapter 6, for all of the data gathered on the causes and effects of poverty in the United States, public debate still pays almost no attention to systematic analysis of changing social systems as a way of substantially alleviating it. Perhaps the main if not only exception to this general pattern is the development of organizational theory as applied to managing corporations, in which systemic problems are in fact often defined and dealt with as such. It is perhaps ironic that a field of study whose roots in this country were firmly planted in concerns about the horrible consequences produced by rapid capitalist industrialization in the late 1800s and early 1900s and the urbanization that went with it should now be most highly developed and appreciated by corporations.

The continuing collective inability to think sociologically has both social and personal consequences. For societies, the effect is felt primarily through the mistaken belief that social problems can be understood and solved as an accumulation of individual troubles and predispositions.[9] This approach is guaranteed to fall short—as we can see in the intractability of most social problems, from poverty to drug use—because a society and the social problems it generates cannot be understood without paying attention to the social facts that underlie them. Good social

---

[8]See Robert K. Merton, "Our Sociological Vernacular," *Columbia* (November 1981):42–44.

[9]For a classic statement on the difference between personal troubles and social issues, see C. Wright Mills, *The Sociological Imagination* (New York: Oxford University Press, 1959), Chapter 1.

consequences in a society are not necessarily the direct result of goodness in people, just as bad consequences are not the result of badness in people. This is not to deny that problems such as racism, sexism, and poverty involve individuals, or that social problems can be solved by paying attention only to social facts and not their individual manifestations. It does suggest, however, that our general inabilty to think in terms of social facts, as well as our preoccupation with the individual, makes it very difficult if not impossible to understand or effectively deal with social problems on a causal level.

Consider, for example, the situation of a community whose water supply is polluted by industrial emissions. People become sick in great numbers and the medical community responds by explaining why: they have toxins in their bodies. An antidote is dispensed to the population. As the population grows, the number of sick people, the manufacture of the antidote, and the size of the medical establishment all grow with it.

It is not inaccurate to define this situation as an individual problem, for it certainly is that on one level. But to act as though the biological system comprising an individual is the only or even most meaningful unit of causal analysis is so narrow and short-sighted that it leads to an endless cycle of disease and treatment that will only grow worse as population and production grow. A second approach might be to install equipment to purify the water, defining the problem on the level of the reservoir as part of an ecological system that includes the community but not the industrial society that produces the pollutants. This is a more effective approach, but only until other effects of air- and rain-borne pollutants are discovered, such as lung cancer, defoliation of forests, contamination of crops, and destruction of other species in the ecosystem. The problem is that it is generally in the nature of systems—whether they be ecosystems or social systems—that their various elements do not have isolated single effects on one another, but interact in complicated ways difficult to identify and deal with on a one-by-one basis.[10]

The most effective solutions are ones that reach farther and farther back in the causal chain and farther and farther out to

---

[10] For a sociological analysis of the consequences of this kind of complexity in highly technological systems such as nuclear power, see Charles Perrow, *Normal Accidents* (New York: Basic Books, 1984).

include larger contexts, in this case extending not only to how factories generate and treat emissions, but to the economic and political systems that allow if not encourage people to value production over a clean environment. Ultimately, the cure for the sick people in the small town may involve a radical change in an entire society's value system as manifested in a way of life and mode of production—in other words, in social facts.

Certainly no social system changes without change occurring among individuals; but it is also true that no system can change through individual change alone. And the larger and more complex the system, the more important systemic change becomes. Unless change also occurs on the collective level of social facts that define the terms and arrangements shaping our lives in relation to one another, then it does not extend far beyond the kind of private, personal solutions usually associated with individual self-improvement—enhanced individual adjustment, functioning, enlightenment, and rewards.[11] Being able to buy bottled water or install expensive home filtration systems are private solutions to a social problem, solutions whose access is limited to a select few (a fact that has its own social explanation and implications). Like all private solutions, they do little if anything to solve the social problem. Indeed, even if everyone in the community could afford to install such devices, the social problem of environmental pollution would remain unsolved; we would have succeeded only in insulating ourselves to some degree from its effects. The causes of the pollution, which extend ultimately to an entire social system, will generate other effects as well, and so long as we respond only at the level of manifestations and proximate causes, we risk remaining trapped in a succession of treatments and insulations that will only be personal solutions for those who can afford them.

At the personal level, sociological thinking enriches psychological understanding by locating individual experiences in their social context. Psychotherapy, for example, is increasingly turning to social contexts to understand and treat emotional problems in individual patients. Individual psychological functioning is not an insulated, self-contained process; it is a response to social circumstances using learned patterns of response derived from lifelong histories of such responses in families, schools, workplaces, and so

---

[11] See C. Wright Mills, op cit., pp. 8–11. What Mills says about problems applies equally well to solutions.

on. It is also necessary to pay attention to the social characteristics that identify us to others. Feminist therapy, for example, is an emerging theoretical framework grounded in the idea that the emotional problems women struggle with are inextricably bound up with their position as females in male-dominated social systems. Similar insights are being explored in relation to characteristics such as race and ethnicity.[12] In short, while psychologists may be able to explain physiological phenomena such as color perception or the biochemistry of nicotine addiction without paying much attention to social systems, they cannot take this limited approach very far when dealing with people as they actually live in the world.

We do not have to engage in sociologically informed psychotherapy, however, to enrich our understanding of individual lives. The more we understand how social systems work and affect those who participate in them, the more we can identify our own behavior and experience as part of recognizable patterns that link us with other people. What we might have identified, for example, as the product of a unique family history may be understood in a larger context as we see how the patterns that constituted family life themselves reflect patterns found in society as a whole, that the emotional problems we struggle with are not simply due to the kind of parents we had, but on a larger level to the characteristics of social systems that shape family life, including parents and their behavior towards children.

In this sense, even the most private uses of sociological insight eventually bring us back to social facts. Movements for social justice—such as the women's and civil rights movements—could not occur until women and blacks redefined their personal troubles as manifestations of social problems that touched all who share their common gender or racial status. Without such awareness, each individual's suffering and deprivation remains isolated from the suffering and deprivation of others without hope of identifying the true causes of what are fundamentally social phenomena.

---

[12]See, for example, the journal *Women and Therapy: A Feminist Quarterly* (New York: The Haworth Press); Miriam Greenspan, *A New Approach to Women and Therapy* (New York: McGraw-Hill, 1983); or Elaine Pinderhughes, *Understanding Race, Ethnicity, and Power: The Key to Efficacy in Clinical Practice* (New York: Free Press, 1989).

One can suspect that the reluctance to think sociologically—grounded in the insistence that the individual is the most meaningful unit of analysis and understanding—indicates something important about the nature of industrial societies and their lack of cohesion, as well as about individuals and their generally weak connection to them. This is particularly true in the United States where the focus on individualism may be greater than at any time or place in human history. Americans are unusually likely to persist in the notion that social problems are caused by individuals—that crime is the result of criminal personalities and the drug problem is simply a failure of individuals to "say no" to drugs; that poverty is the result of laziness, ignorance, and poor training just as wealth is the result of hard work, talent, and higher education; that nuclear power plant accidents happen because individuals make mistakes, not because social systems produce nuclear power plants in the first place. In 1989 a quarter of a million barrels of oil were spilled off the coast of Alaska when an oil tanker ran aground while being piloted by an unlicensed pilot and captained by a man who may have been drinking. The public reaction soon focused on the behavior of the individuals involved which, while certainly not an inappropriate response, ignored the larger question of how systems are structured in ways that make such accidents inevitable regardless of the number of safe-guards.[13] Nor does it raise the still larger question of why huge tankers full of oil—some of which must in the course of things run aground sooner or later—were plying the seas in the first place, of how and why we became a society whose way of life depends so heavily on fuels that must be obtained at such risks to the natural environment.

All of this is a variation on the theme of focusing on the notes to the exclusion of the symphony (not to mention the idea of music itself which transcends the symphony as form. All societies have some form of music as part of their culture, but most do not include symphonies). It is of course true that if, for example, individuals did not choose to take drugs, there would be no drug problem; but to focus on this level of analysis to the exclusion of all others misses the equally obvious point that individuals do not make choices in a vacuum, that most choices are made from socially structured alternatives, and that we also need to understand what it is about

---

[13] See Charles Perrow, *Normal Accidents* (New York: Basic Books, 1984).

the United States that so many of its people, from so many different classes and walks of life, seem so bent upon taking drugs. We can focus on individuals to understand what motivates someone to get high or stoned, but that will not tell us why there are so many more people in this society who want to feel this way than there are in other societies or, for that matter, why there seem to be so many more now than there were in the United States generations ago. The only way to understand that is to understand the social context in which people make these kinds of individual decisions.

The power and the promise of sociological analysis thus lies in its focus on the social contexts in which human life occurs, a focus that more clearly reveals the interaction between individuals and their many kinds of environments, enabling us to affect each as well as the relationships among them. But to move towards this way of looking at the world, we have to acquire the sociological literacy necessary for thinking in terms of social systems and their characteristics.

Sociology promotes awareness by focusing on the fundamental constructs of social life—culture, social structure, population, and human ecology (as well as the hundreds of concepts that derive from them and their application, such as "role" and "group"). These define and set sociology apart as an academic discipline and, beyond academics, as a perspective on human life available to anyone who cares to acquire, cultivate, and apply it. These concepts are fundamental because they define what sociologists would have us pay attention to, just as concepts such as "life" and "cell" help define the perspective of biologists and "personality" helps to define the framework of psychology.

While basic concepts define what we look at, they do not define how we look or how we interpret what we observe. These tasks depend, respectively, on methodology and theory. For the moment, however, this is getting ahead of ourselves, for the questions of "How?" and "Why?" and, perhaps most important, "So?" must wait upon a more detailed answer to the question of "What?"

CHAPTER
TWO

— ♦ —

On

Culture

— ♦ —

Creating
the World

W<small>e</small> tend to think that we live in the world "as it is," that is, as if what we perceive to be real corresponds to some fixed, absolute reality; but one of the most remarkable things about human beings is our collective ability to literally create the world we live in, to make it up from scratch. Most of what goes on around us and, for that matter, inside of us, simply would not exist "as it is" were it not for this ability to socially construct reality. What is most important sociologically is the fact that this ability flows directly from the existence of culture.

Culture, Reality,
and the Discovery of the Self

Culture refers to the accumulated sum of symbols, ideas, and material products associated with life in a social system: the symbols and rules that comprise language; the beliefs, values, attitudes, and norms that form the core from which we perceive, think, feel, and behave; and the meaningful forms that we give to sound, shape, and movement—from music, art, and dance to religious ritual and body language. It also includes the myriad ways in which we shape the physical world, from the vegetable pigments used to paint the body in sacred tribal rituals to the sand from a beach used to fashion silicon chips or the arrangement of flowers and plants that create the unmistakably human order of a garden. We leave our marks everywhere, not least upon ourselves, as we engage in the seemingly unique human endeavor of transforming the world by giving it meaning and value.

What makes all of this possible is the symbol. From numerals, musical notes, and the letters that form words to objects, colors, shapes, and gestures—all have in common that we take them to mean something in addition to what they otherwise are. What makes them cultural is that the meanings we attribute to them are not private—they comprise a collective supply of raw materials from which we create reality—and their authority flows from the authority we invest in society itself. When we give something a name we are in the simplest sense creating its reality for us by establishing a relationship with it. That which is not named is more likely to fall beyond our attention and awareness; which is to say, it does not exist for us. When we name a dot of light in the sky as a "star," we incorporate it into a collective reality, and in that sense, we make it real to us in a way that it otherwise would not be. As a species we are in many ways insulated and isolated from the world around us, prisoners of relatively feeble senses. It is primarily through symbols that we reach out from our isolation to the world, including one another, and establish connections on bridges of meaning.

As the philosopher, Susanne Langer wrote, this ability to create reality lies at the heart of what makes us human:

> Only a small part of reality, for a human being, is what is actually going on; the greater part is what he imagines in connection with the sights and sounds of the moment. . . . It means that his world is bigger than the stimuli which surround him, and the

measure of it is the reach of his coherent and steady imagination. An animal's environment consists of the things that act on his senses. . . . He does not live in a world of unbroken space and time, filled with events even when he is not present or when he is not interested; his "world" has a fragmentary, intermittent existence, arising and collapsing with his activities. A human being's world hangs together, its events fit into each other; no matter how devious their connections, there always are connections, in one big framework of time and space. . . . *The world* is something human.[1]

This is especially true about what we cannot perceive with our senses, but "know" abstractly; that is, what we cannot perceive but nonetheless have named. As an abstraction, "love" cannot be seen in a pure, direct form; only its indirect manifestations are available to us. We can judge from people's behavior whether they love us, but the love is not the behavior itself. The love is a predisposition to behave in certain ways, a set of feelings, perceptions, and judgments of us, none of which we can see. We can talk about the feeling, but the feeling is not the words themselves. And yet we behave as if it were as real as a sidewalk or a piece of fruit, and value it far more highly. Many people organize much of their lives around the problems of understanding and securing love for themselves, in spite of (if not because of) the fact that love is an invisible abstraction.

Unlike love, a quark is something that may potentially be directly perceived, but even in that event, this subatomic particle will most likely exist as an abstraction to most people. Before the word was introduced to name it, whatever it is that "quark" represents had no reality whatsoever for us, yet now it does even for those who never have or ever will see any evidence that they exist. The word is enough. We can now think about particles that are smaller than electrons and neutrons (which we have also never seen), because they became part of our reality when the word connected us to them. And so it is with all words which, like slender threads, connect us to whatever they name, weaving a reality and, in the process, embedding us in it. In this sense, the power of symbols is not simply in marking the world and our experience of it. They are more than a handy cataloging system for

---

[1] Susanne K. Langer, "The Growing Center of Knowledge," in *Philosophical Sketches* (Baltimore: Johns Hopkins Press, 1962), pp. 145–46.

storing and transmitting knowledge; they are also profoundly relational in character, connecting us to the world in a meaningful way. Without them, a great deal of what passes for experience simply would not exist in our memories of what we call the past, our conscious experience of the present, or our wonder about perhaps the greatest of all abstractions, the future.

This extends to the most intimate relationship of all, our connection to the entity we call "self." The nineteenth-century French sociologist Émile Durkheim suggests that the idea of an individual self may be one of the most abstract notions we have ever conceived.[2] What, after all, is it? Can it be seen, touched, smelled, or heard beyond the doings of our bodies? Surely our selves are not our bodies themselves or what they do, although we take all of that to indicate the existence of a self that makes it all happen. The self is an idea about our own existence, an idea that behaviorists such as B. F. Skinner pointed out has no objective reality we can observe scientifically, and is therefore of little scientific interest.[3] And yet, we take the self to be absolutely real in its existence and in its effects. When the body does something that offends, it is the self we hold responsible, not the body.[4] There is no "as if" in our living of the self's existence. We do not live as an abstraction, a notion, a symbolic construct. We live it as concrete reality.

Earlier in this century the American philosopher George Herbert Mead wrote about a process by which, he argued, we discover ourselves as children through our discovery of others.[5] Infants tend to experience the world in an "undifferenti-

---

[2] See, for example, Émile Durkheim, *Sociology and Philosophy* (New York: The Free Press, 1974), and *The Rules of the Sociological Method* (New York: The Free Press, 1938), originally published posthumously, 1924 and 1895 respectively. The former in particular raises questions about the nature of individual and collective life that are at the heart of sociology as a view of the world.

[3] His most well-known statement on this is *Beyond Freedom and Dignity* (New York: Knopf, 1971).

[4] Two interesting exceptions to this are the ways in which men commonly refer to their penises as independent beings with wills of their own and the common nineteenth-century perception of the womb as an independent source of chronic ill health and vulnerability in women. In relation to the latter, see Barbara Ehrenreich and Deidre English, *For Her Own Good: 150 Years of the Experts' Advice to Women* (Garden City, NY: Anchor, 1979).

[5] George Herbert Mead, *Mind, Self, and Society* (Chicago: University of Chicago Press, 1934).

ated oneness," an egocentric state lacking a boundary between the world and selves that divides the world into self and others, according to child psychiatrist Selma Fraiberg.[6] In this state, the infant is unaware that others have a point of view from which they experience and think about themselves and the world. Therefore, the infant is equally unaware that he or she also has a point of view: as far as the infant can tell, things as he or she perceives them are simply things as they are. Unlike an umpire who would say, "I call 'em as I see 'em" or even the one who would say, "I call 'em as they *are*," the infant would more likely say, "Until I call 'em, they *aren't*."

Mead argued that a crucial transition into social life occurs when we discover other people as selves by becoming aware of their inner lives, by realizing that our own behavior is the object of someone else's point of view, that other people have expectations of us, that they perceive and evaluate us in varying ways, have feelings about us, and, perhaps most important, that much of their inner life has nothing to do with us at all. The key to understanding this entire process is the use of language to symbolically mark experience. Language becomes a bridge of meaning that connects our otherwise isolated and insulated experience to the experience of others, and without it, what we know of as ourselves simply would not and could not exist. It is therefore only through language, Mead argues, that we discover ourselves by discovering others, and that we become aware of our point of view *as* a point of view rather than simply as "the way things are."

From this awareness emerges the entity known as self, which we then learn to view as if it were an other. We talk to it, think and have feelings about it, evaluate it, defend and condemn it, struggle to believe in it, scold and praise it, feel proud or ashamed of it, try to get ahold of it, disown it ("I'm not myself today"), seek therapy to accept it, and, often, worry about how we present it to others and how they perceive and respond to it. Our preoccupation with the self reflects how culture enables us to reach not only beyond ourselves, but into ourselves. Paradoxically, the self, which we often perceive in opposition to the constraints imposed by social life, is itself to a considerable degree a cultural crea-

---

[6] For a delightful and insightful view of what the world may look like to infants and young children, see Selma Fraiberg, *The Magic Years* (New York: Scribners, 1959), especially Chapter 4.

tion, not in the sense of being fashioned by some external intelligence, but in the sense that both the "stuff" and the process from which the self emerges are social.

Beliefs

Perhaps the most cultural aspect of the self is our collective belief that it actually exists, an idea we repeatedly reinforce in a variety of ways; even the simple exchanges we make upon greeting one another constitute recognition that we do in fact exist. Even though these rituals are relatively meaningless and sometimes ingenuous (people do not always want to know how we really are), we nonetheless feel badly when people fail to participate.

All cultural ideas have at least one of four different aspects: beliefs, values, attitudes, and norms. Of these, beliefs are perhaps the most fundamental because they make assertions about reality. Any such assertion has a belief aspect, and when its authority is collective rather than individual, it is a cultural belief. The statement "abortion is murder" rests on several beliefs, including that a fetus constitutes a human being from the moment of conception, it is a separate being and not part of its mother's body, and there are different legal categories of killing, depending on how justified the killing is thought to be. The criteria for deciding whether killing is justified, however, focus on the social relationships between those being killed and those doing the killing, as well as their relationships to their societies—all of which are abstract. Every society varies on who is considered a human being and therefore subject to the rights and privileges that go with that standing. Lines are drawn in many different ways, in the process excluding everything from other species to women, foreigners, children, and slaves. At issue here is not some immutable and absolute reality of what constitutes a human being; it is instead the crucial issue of where to draw the boundaries delineating various levels of membership in a social system, boundaries which are and always have been a matter of cultural definition.

The boundaries we draw between humans and other species illustrate the powerful and pervasive effects cultural beliefs can have. Unlike many native American cultures, for example, we insist on distinguishing humans from "other animals," often not looking upon humans as animals at all. There is, we believe, a natural world distinct from the human world. We regard the nest fashioned by a bird or a dam built by beavers as part of the natural world, but not a house built by humans. In every respect the distinction is arbitrary, for in each case a species is using its natural potential to alter the environment in ways that suit what it identifies as its own needs. Our potential to manipulate objects with our opposable thumbs, to master (not to mention to create) the intricacies of physics and engineering, or to value a dwelling that is considered more grand than those occupied by others of our species are no less natural than the ability of beavers to chew tree trunks clean through or to design a sturdy dam or lodge. The fact that so many of our abilities are learned after birth does not make them any less natural, because our ability to learn is simply one more distinguishing characteristic of our species. Everything we do is connected in some way to our biologically rooted potential as homo sapiens.

On one level, this is all obvious, and yet our cultural view of ourselves routinely (if not indignantly) denies this simple fact of existence. But this denial can have disastrous consequences, for it sets us apart in our own minds from the rest of the natural world. It encourages us to live as though we are disconnected from our environment, and we are more likely to act as if we are not subject to the same natural laws and processes that limit other species. We tend to believe we will somehow transcend the consequences of our behavior, that we can pollute the environment, destroy the ozone, and desecrate the land, and although mere "animal" species will be driven to extinction by the changes we initiate, we will survive. Our shared belief that we are not animals fosters a dangerous arrogance that ultimately may threaten our survival. That we do not believe we are animals does not insulate us from the consequences of the fact that we are, and in the process it creates still more dangerous consequences. As W. I. Thomas pointed out some years ago, what we define as real has real consequences whether it is actually true or not.[7]

As the basic material in the social construction of reality, beliefs allow us to perceive and live in the world, at least to some degree, as something obvious and taken for granted. What is obvious is not so much what is true, but what is believed without question in a particular culture. As such, the obvious constitutes— almost by definition—a collective source of blindness because it is unlikely to occur to us that what is obviously true might in fact be

---

[7]W. I. and D. S. Thomas, *The Child in America* (New York: Knopf, 1928), p. 572.

false. In this sense, sociology should be credited with rather than accused of focusing attention on the obvious. The forces in our personal and social lives that do us the most harm are usually not exotic or obtuse, but right under our noses. If only we were not blinded to them by their inclusion in our culture, we could be more aware of them and would be in a better position to do something about them.

Values

While beliefs provide a particular kind of order by distinguishing between what we think of as real and unreal, values distinguish aspects of reality by ranking them in terms of their social desirability. Values have less to do with how things are than with a collective idea about how they ought to be. Values define goals by discerning what is good and bad, or superior and inferior, and as such play a crucial part in the orchestration of human energy and will. Some of the most important consequences of not defining humans as animals, for example, flow from the accompanying value judgment that humans are superior to animals, a judgment in which much of our collective arrogance and blindness towards the rest of the natural world lies. The current controversies surrounding the use of animals for medical research and testing consumer products, such as cosmetics and household cleaners, focus directly on conflicting values about the development of new products for the capitalist market and the importance of human safety on the one hand, and the desirability of not inflicting pain and suffering on nonhuman animals on the other. Defenders of animal testing argue that human safety and product development are more important than the costs to animal subjects, while opponents argue that we underestimate and denigrate the lives of nonhuman species and that alternative, although sometimes less efficient methods are available for achieving the same goals without harming other species (an argument that also highlights the high cultural value we place on economic efficiency). The abortion issue is also profoundly rooted in competing values — between what is perceived as the rights of fetuses, for example, and the rights of women to control their own bodies, or between the right of privacy and the right of communities to control behavior.

Like beliefs, values have an obvious taken-for-granted quality, as if they were natural rather than cultural constructions. We tend to experience wants, desires, and preferences in what seems to be such a direct and unmediated way that it rarely occurs to us that they reflect the cultural environment rather than something inherent in ourselves as individuals, and that the depth with which we experience them has to do more with the power and efficiency of socialization than with human nature. It is true, of course, that not all notions of what is preferable derive from cultural values. Even newborn infants prefer warmth to cold, satiation to hunger, and touch and loving talk to isolation or violence. As fundamental as these "hard-wired" preferences are, however, they cannot begin to explain the richness, complexity, and conflict found in cultural value systems.

Given how deeply values are felt, it is easy (as well as self-confirming) to ascribe values to people in general, especially as attributes of human nature. Since Americans, for example, value a steadily increasing standard of living, we assume that everyone wants to consume more each year and accumulate possessions, and that this is a central human value. The same might be said about the preoccupation with romantic love, one of the central organizing principles of life in the United States (popular music, for example, seems to have little else as its subject). Trapped in our own ethnocentrism, it seems peculiar if not alien to imagine societies in which acquiring ever-mounting quantities of goods is not valued or in which romantic love is either far less important (as in most preindustrial societies) or virtually nonexistent (which seems to have been the case prior to the age of chivalry, at least in relation to marriage).[8] Even more remote is the idea that romantic love and materialism may be linked, that the high value we place on looking to another person to complete ourselves, make our dreams come true, and compensate for all of life's disappointments and deprivations may have something to do with our mode of production, alienation in the workplace, the loss of a strong sense of family and community, and the incessant message that the road to happiness lies through consumption and material acquisition. And, if that does not suffice, as it is bound not to, we are deluded into finding that particular someone who can make up for if not substitute for it all, which is also bound not to work.

The profound influence of cultural values in almost every

---

[8] For a history of romantic love, see Denis De Rougement, *Love in the Western World*, trans. Montgomery Belgion (Princeton, NJ: Princeton University Press, 1983).

decision we make coupled with the relative invisibility of these values as cultural phenomena raises difficult questions about the whole idea that doing what we want can ever be an exercise in free choice. As Schopenhauer put it, "We want what we will, but we don't will what we want."[9] In this sense, to explain a behavior as being what someone wants and chooses freely suggests that the source of our wants and, therefore, responsibility for what we do rests solely with ourselves, that we are self-generated and regulated. A common defense of pornography and prostitution, for example, is that women choose to participate, just as some battered women choose to remain with their husbands in spite of the abuse. But in what sense do we exercise free will when the alternatives are socially structured and not of our own creation, and as well, we are socialized to prefer some alternatives to others or blinded to many alternatives altogether? Is it free will for women to choose degrading or abusive situations when they live in a society where women are generally treated as second-class citizens, routinely dominated, terrorized, harassed, degraded, abused, discriminated against, and discouraged from developing financial independence?[10] If women tend to have self-images compatible with degrading work, in what sense can we attribute their decisions entirely to their own personal wants, desires, and preferences?

Similar observations can be made about the entire range of preferences that dominate decision making in everyday life. Whether we want to smell "good" by masking natural body odors with chemicals, value college education, or believe in national military superiority, we tend to mistake the narrow confines of cultural values for universal human experiences of choice and alternatives. In doing so, we deprive ourselves of much of our potential latitude to make free choices by stepping outside of cultural boundaries and seeing alternatives. To reach these conclusions, of course, we draw on yet another cultural value, for critically examining a social environment to create new alternatives

---

[9] Quoted in Marvin Harris, *Cultural Materialism*, (New York: Random House, 1979), p. 60.

[10] See, for example, Susan Brownmiller, *Against Our Will: Men, Women, and Rape* (New York: Simon and Schuster, 1975); Andrea Dworkin, *Women Hating* (New York: E.P. Dutton, 1974); Laura Lederer, *Take Back the Night: Women on Pornography* (New York: William Morrow, 1980); and Diana E. H. Russell, *Sexual Exploitation: Rape, Child Sexual Abuse, and Workplace Harassment* (Beverly Hills, CA: Sage, 1984).

is itself part of our culture. One way to interpret this is to say that culture is a closed system and no matter what doors we go through, we cannot escape it. But a more revealing interpretation is that culture provides the potential to transcend itself. It is as if culture is a tunnel that, while confining our vision within its walls, also goes someplace and each direction we follow through it (and much of what we discover as a result) becomes part of the tunnel. In this sense, culture is both means and end, extending and limiting our experience and vision at the same time.

It is tempting, on the other hand, to make too much of the idea that our values and consequent behavior have their roots in the cultural environment. Since most of our behavior is mediated to some degree by culture, one might argue that the concept of personal responsibility itself is based on a false premise of human self-determination and free will, and that no one, therefore, is responsible for anything. But just as the notion that we are self-contained creatures whose lives go on independent of our environment exaggerates our autonomy, so too, the idea that we are mere puppets dangling by cultural strings greatly understates our ability to create and defy. We are more like jazz improvisers who draw upon technical training in music, from the notation that gives music its language to concepts such as major and minor, riff, blues, swing, straight-ahead, and bebop to different musical forms such as the song. Like musicians, we learn cultural forms that in the learning limit our thinking and, therefore, action; but within the *general* limitations of musical form we bend, distort, twist, and break the rules in specific situations and ways, and it is this that gives both jazz improvisation and human life their unmistakable character. They have the potential to be innovative and yet familiar.

In addition to confusing the relationship between the individual and culture, we tend to think solely in terms of that relationship, as if culture is the hub of a wheel around which individuals revolve as independent spokes joined only to the center. This draws attention to the effect of culture on each individual, which we are typically aware of only when we feel prevented from doing what we want—when, as Schopenhauer reminds us, the study of cultural values suggests that the most profound cultural limitations operate just at those moments when we are doing exactly what we want because it is then that we are least aware of the power of cultural constraints. When we focus on the relationship between the individual and culture, however, we often fail to see that the most important connections are those among people. A culturally-based preoccupation with individuals, which leads us to see them as living independently of or in constant rebellion against cultural constraints, is linked to the related view that we can live independently from one another. Yet the importance of culture lies not so much in the constraints it exerts on individual autonomy but in the ways it brings us together by rendering us and what we think, feel, and do as identifiable and familiar to one another.

As a common medium in which we find ourselves, culture is not external to us individually or collectively; it is among and of us, and by participating in it, by living our improvised lives within the limitations of its various forms, we also participate in one another's lives. Because culture exists through us and we through it, there is no boundary separating us from it and, therefore, no boundaries separating those who live together in a society. Culture is like the air. It is everywhere; we cannot live without it. And, most importantly, it is in a relationship of such continuing exchange, flowing in and out of us, that it would be arbitrary to delineate any lines between us and it. The air is at once outside our bodies and yet in every cell; our skin is simply a membrane that regulates the flow. We are of the air, but in a particular form. And since we all share this relationship with the air, we are all of one another, as well, for the air of which you are a part is the same air of which everyone else is a part.

But, of course, we do not live with this awareness from moment to moment, which is itself a product of culture, for inherent in all cultures is a partial blindness to their own existence and workings. When applied to other cultures, this awareness takes the form of ethnocentrism, the tendency to view other cultures with the same kind of undifferentiated, egocentric one-ness through which infants perceive the world. Unlike infantile egocentrism, however, ethnocentrism involves value judgments ranking one's own culture as superior to all others, and in the process rests on the arrogant, often unarticulated assumption that other cultural frameworks are mostly wrong or functionally inadequate.

It was ethnocentrism that led Europeans to characterize the Americas as the New World and to conquer and exploit tribal societies; and ethnocentrism is basic to celebrating the "discovery" of America by Columbus thousands of years after it was truly discovered by migrants who made their way from Siberia to Alaska. When white Australians held a bicentennial celebration of the "founding" of Australia in 1988, counterdemonstrations by various tribal groups protested the ethnocentrism that ignored the aboriginal cultures whose presence preceded the Europeans by some 40,000 years. But to avoid the false impression that ethnocentrism is a purely European malady, consider the Japanese, who greeted the first shipwrecked white sailors who washed upon their shores as barbarians and often treated them accordingly by promptly executing them.

This culturally-induced blindness seems to inhere in all societies, and in the form of ethnocentrism, it is particularly suited to ideological and political purposes. Fear of and hostility towards outsiders has long been an effective method for rallying a disenchanted populace behind a faltering national leadership. In some cases—such as the persecution of Jews in Nazi Germany and pogroms in many Eastern European societies over many centuries—groups within societies are identified as outsiders and treated with the kind of blind judgments that characterize ethnocentrism at its worst.

Ethnocentrism is most dangerous, however, not as a cynical tool used by politicians, but as a genuine source of collective and individual blindness. Any serious student of history is bound to be impressed by the astonishing consistency with which political leaders fail to learn from their own mistakes, make what seem to be the most shortsighted decisions, and often seem incapable of seeing what is right under their own noses. It is tempting to rail against them as just so many self-serving incompetents. Their behavior is far more reflective of their social environment than we might like to think, however, for their failure of vision often reflects the ethnocentric assumptions of their culture.

The United States became embroiled in the Vietnam War largely by failing to understand the social forces involved in what began as a war against colonialism (a goal that it supported in the aftermath of World War II) led by Ho Chi Minh, a leader who embraced many of the fundamental principles of U.S. democracy and was eager to maintain ties with the United States. As James Gibson argues, however, the U.S. government was blinded by the assumption that political movements that in any way associate themselves with Marxist analysis or communist ideology are both unnatural and imposed from the outside (usually the Soviet Union or China).[11] The "obvious" facts that the Vietnamese were fighting French colonialism which was a direct outgrowth of capitalist-based imperialism, and that it was not unreasonable to use Marxist analysis as a framework for both making sense of their situation as well as changing it, seems to have been so deeply obscured by ethnocentrism that the U.S. leadership simply could not see it.[12]

The actual conduct of the war also illustrates the dangers inherent in a one-sided view of other societies. Most people in the U.S., for example, would agree that nothing increases a sense of national defiance as much as threats by outsiders, and yet the U.S. government persisted in the belief (a belief that was certainly predicated in part on an assumption of Asian inferiority) that punishment would be enough to force the Vietnamese to surrender their deeply held values and abandon a cause they had been defending for decades. U.S. leaders clung to the conviction that if Vietnamese opposition was made to suffer enough, if enough people were killed and maimed and enough communities destroyed, they would give up. As history has recorded, of course, the U.S. could not have been more mistaken. Military might enabled it to win virtually every battle of arms, but it made little difference in the end.

What is perhaps most telling about this fundamental miscalculation is that it had such recent and glaring precedents. Hitler made the same mistake in trying to pound England into submission during the Battle of Britain in the early years of World War II, as the Allies did a few years later when they attempted to subdue Germany by saturation bombing of major population centers.[13] But as we found, even the weakest countries are capable of an astonishing willingness to undergo extreme hardship at the cost of defying nations far more powerful then they.

Because what we consider to be concrete reality is so

---

[11] James Gibson, *The Perfect War* (New York: Vintage, 1989).

[12] For a balanced, comprehensive, and well-written history of the war in Vietnam, see Stanley Karnow, *Vietnam: A History* (New York: Viking Press, 1983). For a fascinating historical view of the blunders that societies make even when viable alternatives are readily available, see Barbara Tuchman, *The March of Folly: From Troy to Vietnam* (New York: Alfred Knopf, 1984).

[13] Sociologists were among those who documented the ineffectiveness of saturation bombing. See I. L. Janis, *Air War and Emotional Stress* (New York: McGraw-Hill, 1951). For a more recent treatment of similar issues, see R. E. Neustadt and E. R. May, *Thinking in Time* (New York: The Free Press, 1986).

profoundly affected by cultural beliefs and values, to a great extent we live out our *idea* of our lives. In Vietnam the United States waged war not against the communists, but against a cultural idea of them, just as the communists waged war against their cultural idea of the U.S. A central sociological problem of all social life is, then, to be aware of the beliefs and values we live by and the consequences they create; and, from there, to conceive of and appreciate alternatives.

Norms, Morality, and Deviance

Value systems are inherently problematic because they serve only as guidelines for making choices. Social psychologist Roger Brown likens them to a grammar that we use to construct or interpret sentences we have never encountered before.[14] When two or more important values are invoked by the same social situation, the resulting conflict reflects the imprecision and ambiguity inherent in even the most rigid value system. Certainly the value placed on honesty is one of the highest in our culture, for example, and yet at times it may conflict with the equally high value placed on loyalty to family or friends. There is no definitive rule that tells us what to do in the face of such choices, especially given the endless number of possible situations in which they might occur.

The importance of value conflicts, of course, lies not merely in their philosophical significance but in the ways people choose to behave as a result. Since every social system depends to a considerable degree on the ability to regulate behavior, and since value systems are at best a loose set of guidelines, they cannot do the job by themselves. The regulation of behavior, from preventing sexual violence against women to promoting hard work and honesty, must rely on specific ideas focusing not simply on what is good and desirable (as values do) but on what is expected and required. The result is a normative system which enforces standards of appearance and behavior.

The difference between what is desired and what is required is sanctions—the rewards and punishments that norms attach to specific appearances and behaviors. Values are simply ideas about how people ought to behave, while norms go a step further by

---

[14] Roger Brown, *Social Psychology* (New York: The Free Press, 1965), p. 407.

connecting appearance and behavior to social consequences, from a stern look to the death penalty. If terrorists plant a bomb that blows up a hydroelectric plant, there are many objective results—physical damage to the plant and the consequent disruption of people's lives, economic losses, and so forth. When they are identified as the perpetrators, however, there are additional consequences that depend not on what they did, but on the sanctions the normative system attaches to it. These consequences are somewhat arbitrary since they are produced not by the behavior but by a cultural system of ideas. As such, they depend greatly on the social situation in which people act and the norms that apply to it.

If, for example, the bombers were extortionists who blew up the plant because the authorities refused to pay them a huge sum of money to finance their retirement in the South Seas, they could expect severe punishment. But if they acted as saboteurs during wartime, although their enemies might execute them, their home country might confer high honors on them. The fact that neither of these consequences is inherent in the behavior itself is what gives norms their culturally "synthetic" quality (and, when comparing cultures, their "relative" quality), for they literally create consequences that would not otherwise exist.

The synthetic quality of norms is probably most apparent in physical appearances. Someone who goes out for walks while naked and in full view of the neighbors may risk objective consequences such as catching cold (or a sunburn), or of revealing their naked appearance to others. As everyone knows, however, the social consequences would be far more severe (except, of course, in nudist colonies where people are not allowed to walk about *with* clothes). I was once camping near a remote Vermont lake when this peculiar quality of norms became apparent to me as I prepared to go swimming. I found myself standing in a beautiful grove of birch trees with no one but my wife for miles around, taking off my clothes and about to put on a bathing suit. Suddenly, with one foot in and one foot out, the question occurred to me, "Why am I putting this on?" and lacking a convincing reply, I took a rare skinny-dip that once again impressed me with the power of cultural norms to constrain even the simplest of human experiences.

Why do societies find it necessary to construct synthetic consequences that often lack a compelling practical reason for their existence? Why should it matter so deeply to many people (who all began life unself-consciously naked) whether we wear clothes or not? Or, for that matter, why should we feel justified in seriously injuring if not killing someone who has stolen and is running away with a replaceable object such as a television that we have defined as our "private property"? The answer to such questions depends on your general view of what societies are about; and sociology provides at least two answers.[15]

From what is known as the functional perspective, norms and values exist because social systems could not operate without them. Social systems are composed of social relationships consisting largely of the expectations people have of one another. Since norms and values are cultural ideas on which expectations are based, they are, almost by definition, an integral part of every social system.

In a deeper and less mundane sense, normative systems and their associated values define the boundaries of groups, communities, and societies. Members of a community are those who adhere to shared standards of appearance and behavior, and by these they are known and know themselves. Support for those standards—even through the most passive conformity—affirms both the community in which they are grounded and membership in it. Violation of them endangers to some degree the sense of belonging and acceptance by others, a risk with far more serious consequences than many more concrete forms of punishment. Conformity to norms is one of the surest ways for a new member to gain acceptance and influence in a group, and deviance is among the surest ways to be stubbornly refused, even when people have a great deal to offer in other ways.[16] Norms are a particularly important part of group boundaries because they focus on the visible manifestations of beliefs and values. Acceptance as group members does not depend on subscribing to the appropriate values and beliefs; it depends on the ability to seem to subscribe by our appearance and behavior, including what we say with speech and body language.

From this perspective, the actual content of normative systems

[15] These will be discussed in Chapter 5.

[16] See, for example, some of the research on influence in small groups found in E. P. Hollander, "Competence and Conformity in the Acceptance of Influence," *Journal of Abnormal and Social Psychology* 51 (1960): 365–69; and C. L. Ridgeway, "Nonconformity, Competence, and Influence in Groups," *American Sociological Review* 46 (June 1981): 333–47.

is secondary to simply having *a* normative system. Societies are not unlike groups of children who, when they form a club make up a name and a set of rules, especially those that define membership. To have a club without rules is unthinkable, even if they are nonsensical, silly, self-contradictory, or cruel. It doesn't really matter so long as they have *some* rules, for when they create a normative system they are in effect establishing the identity of their social system and, to the degree that they value their membership in it, their own identities as well.

Durkheim believed that this collective identity lies at the foundation of social life and is the primary constraining force that societies exert on their members.[17] It is, he argued, the true seat of morality; indeed, morality in its most important sense consists not of specific rules about behavior but the overall shared sense of what a society and membership in it are all about, from which such rules draw their authority. Moral questions are those that concern who we are in a collective sense, which means that moral debates are not only about whether specific behaviors should be allowed, but also (and more profoundly) about how communities will think of and define themselves. At the level of societies, the most morally important aspect of social life is not behavior per se, but the feeling of attachment and identification that binds people to society, from which everything else of social importance flows, including behavior. Society itself is the overriding moral entity.

From this perspective, deviance is not simply the breaking of rules, but a violation of social boundaries that raises questions about the standing of the offender as a member. A man who wears jeans to his job as an insurance executive does far more than violate a dress code; he also inspires doubts about his commitment to the collective "us" that morality is all about. This is true of all deviance from the most mundane folkways, such as facing front in elevators or refraining from belching loudly at the dinner table, to the most deeply held moral codes governing murder, treason, and incest. In this sense, *all* norms and their violation have to do with belonging and commitment, and are the basis of identity in both social systems and individuals.

If morality has to do fundamentally with belonging, it follows that people who are defined as outsiders will be treated as deviants, and this is in fact the case. This is particularly true in the

---

[17] See Émile Durkheim, *Sociology and Philosophy,* op. cit.

case of stigmatization, when people are treated as deviant not because of what they have done but because of who they are.[18] People who are physically disabled or disfigured, or who have diseases such as AIDS, or who are even related by kinship or friendship to people considered deviant can themselves be treated as deviants who, if they are not actually punished, are at least denied the rewards of full group membership.

In some societies, entire categories of people are treated as deviant, including those defined by race, gender, religion, and ethnicity. One of the most paradoxical cases of this is the treatment of females who, while clearly being integral and necessary members of every society, are often treated as deviants.[19] For centuries women have been regarded as incomplete, flawed versions of men, with constitutions that render them weak and below the physical, emotional, and mental standards expected of a normal, healthy human being. In patriarchal societies dominated by masculine values, women cannot escape being viewed as outsiders at least to some degree. The modern liberal women's movement is in large part a struggle to include women in a male-dominated world, to assure their acceptance as full members of society—in other words, to shed the deviant status that excludes them from full participation and standing and causes them not only to be denied rewards, but subjects them to various forms of punishment from sexual violence, battery, and harassment to more subtle forms of misogyny such as degrading and exploitative media portrayals.[20]

In stark contrast to the goals of liberal feminism, radical feminism rejects women's deviant status by rejecting the patriarchal society that assigns them to it. They have created subcultures in which femaleness is highly valued as a central aspect of social organization. For these women, the cost of admission to main-

---

[18] See Erving Goffman, *Stigma: Notes on the Management of a Spoiled Identity* (Englewood Cliffs, NJ: Prentice-Hall, 1963).

[19] See, for example, Edwin Schur, *Labeling Women Deviant: Gender, Stigma, and Social Control* (New York: Random House, 1984). See also Barbara Ehrenreich and Deirdre English, *For Her Own Good: 150 Years of Experts' Advice to Women* (Garden City, NY: Anchor, 1979) for a fascinating history of the medical aspects of women's status as deviant.

[20] For more on this, see Erving Goffman, *Gender Advertisements* (New York: Harper Colophon, 1976); Lederer, op. cit.; and Diane Barthel, *Putting on Appearances: Gender and Advertising* (Philadelphia: Temple University Press, 1989).

stream patriarchal society includes accepting an identity they find unacceptable in both its traditional and liberal forms, which leaves them with the difficult alternative of redefining important aspects of their identities and creating a separate environment that will support them. In the process, they must to varying degrees insulate themselves from and tolerate the punishments and withholding of rewards (which may include some basic civil rights) that reflect their deviant standing in the surrounding society.

The systematic way that deviance is used to exclude, dominate, exploit, and oppress entire social categories suggests that normative systems have to do with much more than the requirements of social systems. What has come to be referred to as the conflict perspective focuses on the fact that many social systems are marked by struggle over the unequal distribution of wealth, prestige, power, and other resources and rewards. As conflict theorists point out, one of the resources distributed unequally in stratified societies is control over culture, including values and the defining of norms that enforce them. This means that privileged groups have the potential to shape cultural ideas to suit their own interests, including the protection of their privileges which often rest on the exploitation if not the oppression of others.

Consider, for example, values and norms that concern private property. The idea of private property, especially as applied to land and capital, is a relatively recent one in human history, going back perhaps no more than five to seven thousand years; and the idea of accumulating private property as a social value is far more recent than that. Many American Indian tribes viewed land as a part of nature that is beyond human proprietary rights. When whites settled on the island of Nantucket off the coast of Massachusetts, they "purchased" land from the natives who lived there. The Indians were dumbfounded at the subsequent behavior of the new "owners," including the arrest and punishment of Indians who "trespassed" on land that no longer "belonged" to them. The cultural framework of the Indian society simply had no place for such notions, and eventually died out without ever acquiring one.

Of course the norms that protect private property serve the interests of those who own it in direct proportion to how much they have. But such norms assume far more importance when the unequal distribution of property—such as capital—is a basis for inequalities of power, for then the protection of property and its accumulation can easily become the protection of the concentration of power and all of the potential for abuse, exploitation, and oppression that goes with it. In the United States, as in most industrial capitalist societies, the vast majority of capital and other wealth is owned by a tiny minority. The wealthiest one percent of all U.S. families, for example, owned almost 40 percent of all assets, including 60 percent of all corporate stock and 66 percent of all business assets in 1983. The wealthiest ten percent owned 89 percent of stock and 94 percent of business assets.[21]

This kind of accounting does not mean that norms and values that protect private property exist solely to serve elite interests, but it does mean that while they protect our cars, cash, and VCRs, their far greater social effect is the protection of the elite's social dominance and helps to perpetuate the difficult conditions faced by all lower- and working-class households and families as well as many who consider themselves to be middle-class.

Although there are many ways in which the culture of a society affects everyone in relatively uniform ways, its effects depend a great deal on the positions that people occupy. Whites growing up in the rural hinterlands of Wyoming, for example, will not experience American culture in exactly the same ways as Asian-Americans growing up in New York City's Chinatown or African-Americans growing up near the Mississippi Delta or Italian-Americans growing up in Boston's North End. In similar ways, social positions defined by characteristics such as class, occupation, education, religion, gender, and age all affect the elements of culture that we perceive as most salient. It is therefore important when trying to understand any aspect of social environments to pay attention not only to its effects on the entire social system, but also to its differential effects on people who are placed differently in those systems. Ignoring the former deprives us of a

---

[21] Assets include real estate, cash, stocks, bonds, savings, trusts, insurance policies, and business assets. Gathering reliable data on the wealth holdings of the U.S. elite is always a challenge for researchers, and studies tend, if anything, to underestimate the concentration of wealth and power. The source here is an unusually thorough study reported in Democratic Staff of the Joint Economic Committee of the U.S. Congress, *The Concentration of Wealth in the United States* (Washington, DC: Joint Economic Committee, July 1986), Table 2.

full understanding of how social systems work, while ignoring the latter means that whatever understanding we achieve loses much of its human significance.

Attitudes

Beliefs, values, and norms are perhaps that most important of all cultural ideas, for they are primary components in the social construction of reality and the regulation of behavior. Cultural systems would be incomplete, however, without a fourth type of idea—the attitude—which involves emotion. Attitudes are important both because they include emotions that are derived from social life and because they regulate the expression of feelings in different social situations.

Although there are primary emotions such as fear inherent in our species, there are a great many that probably would not exist if not for the social nature of human life. Contempt and disgust, for example, involve judgments about meaning and value, and are quite different from simple dislike and distaste. Infants will screw up their faces with displeasure and spit out bitter or sour food, but this is not the same as a Western adult's reaction who, while chewing on a succulent piece of meat, suddenly learns that it was once part of a dog (a reaction of disgust that would contrast sharply with the approval and pleasure of members of many Asian societies). The centrality of meaning and value is also apparent in emotions such as pride, shame, guilt, love, hate, loyalty, reverence, respect and disrespect, haughtiness, humility, pity, patriotism, sympathy, empathy, and gratitude. All of these are either based on cultural beliefs and values, or have people in social relationships as their object. Without a social context conditioned and mediated by shared ideas, it is difficult to imagine how they might emerge into human experience.

Attitudes predispose us to feel and, therefore, to act in certain ways, depending on the object of our feelings and the social situation in which we find ourselves; but underlying the feelings are beliefs and values that elicit and in many cases legitimize them. Perhaps the most extensively studied attitude is prejudice, for more than any other it is systematically applied to relations between groups, producing undesirable consequences. Feelings of superiority and inferiority associated with race and gender, for example, are based on stereotyped beliefs and values that rank those beliefs in a hierarchy. Men are believed to be more rational and less emotionally expressive than women, and when this belief is placed in the context of a patriarchal value system that ranks rationality and control more highly than nonrationality and emotional expression, men are objects of respect and women are objects of disrespect if not contempt.

Given how often feelings override other considerations in determining how we behave and make decisions, it is striking that so little sociological work has been done in this area.[22] This may be due in part to the fact that emotion is a phenomenon most often associated with psychology and has, therefore, not occurred to most sociologists as a proper area of study. It is also possible that the dominance of the scientific method in the social sciences has made it difficult to study emotion, although one has to wonder why emotion should be so inaccessible to scientific inquiry when mainstream sociology has no apparent trouble studying such inherently abstract notions as culture and, for that matter, prejudice.

One can suspect, however, that the cultural beliefs we hold about emotion and its low standing in our value system also have something to do with its relative invisibility and neglect in sociological studies. We live in a society in which a high value is placed on control, linear predictability, and invulnerability, all of which are difficult to maintain if we allow ourselves the full play of our feelings. In addition, emotional expression is most closely associated with being female, and anyone who wants to achieve a position of influence must to some degree guard against being overly identified with femininity. It is certainly no accident that the cultural stereotype of women as unreliable, unpredictable, vulnerable, weak, and socially unimportant has a close parallel in our general views about emotions. Just as social scientists have paid relatively little attention to such "feminine" areas of life as the family and socialization, so too have they attached relatively little importance to emotional life.

Underlying this bias is an assumption that emotions are relatively unimportant and irrelevant beyond the intimate, female-dominated sphere of private life because in the wider, more public

---

[22] In fact, it was only as recently as the late 1980s that the American Sociological Association formed a section on the sociology of emotion. See, for example, David Franks and E. Doyle McCarthy, eds., *The Sociology of Emotions* (Greenwich, CT: JAI Press, 1988).

world, emotion is perceived as taking a back seat to logic and rational control. The meaning of "attitude" even as a technical term in sociology usually refers to people's opinions on various issues—in other words, to what they think more than what they feel. Even if we pointedly ask people how they *feel* about an issue, they almost always respond with what they think, not what they feel (and more than one person has looked at me quizzically and asked, "What's the difference?" or responded with impatience, as if I was splitting hairs).

A major problem here lies in the mistaken belief that it is possible to live beyond the reach of emotion. When we character-ize people as unemotional or dispassionate, it suggests that they have somehow transcended emotion and operate in a different dimension (or, if one is thinking hierarchically, as we so often do, to say "on a different level," presumably a higher level). While it is possible to be inexpressive to varying degrees, however, there is no such thing as being unemotional. We can always be described in terms of our emotional condition, and unemotional and unfeeling are no less descriptions of emotional states than the terms hysterical or enraged. If we believe that it is possible to be unemotional, we are left in the bizarre position of concluding that the behavior of someone like Adolf Eichmann—whose banal efficiency characterized his participation in the murder of millions during the Holocaust—had nothing to do with his emotional life. It would lead us to believe that when military leaders talk calmly and objectively of the possibility of winning a war in which tens of millions of people are killed in an exchange of nuclear weapons, that we are not hearing the effects of emotion on human behavior and decision making.

It makes more sense to argue that a studied attempt to maintain an emotional condition of flatness, inexpressiveness, detachment, and disconnected awareness of underlying feelings is in itself an emotional phenomenon with profoundly important personal and social consequences, and, that those who make decisions while suppressing awareness or expression of their feelings are in fact engaging in a highly emotional act which should be recognized as such. This is especially problematic in a society where the ability to create this impression is a necessary condition for occupying positions of authority. And if history is any guide, it is an authority that is all too readily abused, with disastrous consequences.

The studied attempt to flatten emotional awareness and expression is a socially regulated psychological state reflecting attitudes associated with different social actors in different situations. We are probably most aware of this social orchestration of emotion when our feelings run contrary to a situation we find ourselves in—when seized with an irrepressible urge to laugh out loud during a funeral, for example, or when a man feels frightened in a situation in which masculinity dictates that he be brave and unflinching (or when a woman feels brave and unflinching in a situation in which she is expected to back down, defer, and otherwise cower in the face of danger).

Strictly speaking, the problem is not how we feel, but how we identify and regulate the expression of feeling. The two are easily confused, however. We are often told to stop feeling something because others find its expression uncomfortable or inappropriate, and the request more often than not focuses on the feeling itself ("There's nothing to be afraid of," and so on). For children this is especially confusing, since feelings cannot be controlled in the way that behavior can be. If we are raised to see no difference between wanting to run away and actually running away, we are not only shaping our behavior to fit social situations, but shaping our inner lives as well. If nothing else, psychotherapy has taught us that our inner lives cannot be shaped in this way without incurring a considerable cost to our emotional health and psychological integrity. Emotions may be repressed, but this only directs them to other forms of expression.

The effects of confusing feeling with behavior go beyond the individual—through our emotions we bring much of what we have to offer to the interaction between individuals and social systems. Social systems, like individuals, are not static; they are a process of constant development and change, and each of us brings emotional energy to that process. If the energy flow is systematically curtailed and restricted to conform to norms, a major source of dynamic change is lost. The systematic denial of inappropriate emotions and their expression is connected to the systematic denial of the social importance of emotion itself, which denies us a major source of human wisdom. The result may include leaders who are so frightened of their own feelings of fear, weakness, doubt, and vulnerability that they cannot make use of them in understanding and guiding their own behavior.

The neglect of attitudes, then, may reflect a deeper patriarchal ambivalence about emotion that views it as important among women and children, and suspect everywhere else. But in the denial of emotion lies not only a distrust of feelings as a basis for action, but a distrust of and disconnection from ourselves and, ultimately, from one another and social systems themselves.

Material Culture

As suggested before, in many important ways a society can be likened to a jazz orchestra in which improvisation is the rule, not the exception. Even with jazz, however, there must be a shared definition and understanding of music—from the simplest notation of flats, sharps, and rests to the more complex structural notions that define different types of composition. Jazz musicians cannot simply do whatever they want; they are always constrained to some degree by the form of the piece they are playing—from the number of bars it contains to its key and chordal structure. Beneath what to the casual listener may seem an unrestrained, free-wheeling succession of notes is an unarticulated inner discipline that gives the entire work its integrity, its *social* integrity as a common enterprise among musicians. Without some shared understanding, there could be no connection among the players or between the players and their audience. There would, in short, be only sound (moving air) not music.

Cultural symbols and ideas are absolutely necessary to make music, for they define not only music itself, but the shared understandings that enable us to make music in *relation* to one another. They are not in themselves enough, however, for music also has a material basis for its existence, from the paper on which music is printed to the brass, wood, and other materials from which instruments are made. In industrial societies we now add to these basic necessities the complex hardware of musical production and reproduction, from microphones, mixers, and tape recorders to electronic instruments, synthesizers, drum machines, and compact disks. In other words, to understand the production of music in any society, we have to pay attention to both material and nonmaterial aspects of culture.

Material culture reflects what seems to be our inherent tendency to transform nature, to turn one thing into another, an ability that lies at the heart of human life and most distinguishes it from that other species. In the most obvious sense, material culture is important because it directly affects the nature and quality of human life, from extending the abilities to see and hear, to creating problems such as pollution and warfare. On a deeper, more analytical level, material culture is sociologically important because it affects the terms on which social life is lived, because material existence has a reciprocal relationship with perceptions of reality, values, feelings, and social expectations, and as well, with the structure of social relationships. The invention of movable type by Gutenberg in the fifteenth century, for example, prompted a social revolution by making it possible for the first time to reproduce and distribute ideas in written form to a vast audience. Widespread literacy suddenly made sense in a way that was unthinkable before that, when only the privileged few had access to precious books. With literacy came the rapid dissemination of ideas and information, greatly increasing the speed of innovation and the development of science and critical thought.

The printing press is, of course, just a machine, a collection of parts arranged in a certain relation to one another, and its social importance depends entirely on what is done with it—in particular, on the kinds of ideas and information people choose to print. The close connection between perception, thought, and feelings on the one hand and behavior on the other made it inevitable that the printing press would become a focus of power struggles for control over the flow of information and ideas. All governments, from the most repressive dictatorship to democracies, try to control printing and publishing during times of crisis by limiting access to presses, mimeograph machines, and even typewriters. In 1983 the government of Romania passed laws requiring owners of typewriters to register them with the police—including a sample of the machine's print—so that the authorities could identify the origin of any publication not to their liking. Those with criminal records or who were deemed to pose "a danger to public order and security" were barred from owning typewriters altogether.[23] In less authoritarian countries, such as the United States, the state has less control over printing and publishing, but it is nonetheless limited largely to those who can afford the technology. As Michael Parenti put it, freedom of the press exists primarily for those who own the presses[24] or who have the money to purchase space in them to

---

[23] *New York Times,* April 24, 1983.

[24] See Michael Parenti, *Inventing Reality* (New York: St. Martin's Press, 1985).

promote themselves. Corporations, unions, and other large organizations are not only able to purchase full-page advertisements in newspapers and magazines, but have recently been allowed to purchase space on the editorial pages of major newspapers.

While the state always has the potential to limit political freedom—of which we are often reminded—we tend to be less aware of how the concentrated economic power of conglomerates and media giants threatens to control the dissemination of ideas for their own interests, including the increase and perpetuation of their own power. In the United States, just ten corporations control among them the NBC, ABC, and CBS radio and television networks, 34 affiliated television stations, more than 200 cable television franchises, 59 magazines, including *Newsweek* and *Time*, 20 record companies, 41 book publishers, and 58 newspapers, including the *Wall Street Journal*, the *Washington Post*, the *Los Angeles Times*, and the *New York Times*.[25] In 1989 media giants Time, Inc. and Warner Communications merged to form the world's largest and most powerful media conglomerate, whose holdings include publishing, music, film, television, and mass market print media. Under the control of such organizations, what appear to be diverse independent sources of news, ideas, art, and music are in fact subject to unitary control and purpose. As one commentator put it:

> Watch a Little, Brown book become a Book of the Month Club pick, a Warner paperback and a Warner Brothers film that is featured in *People,* reviewed in *Time,* with a soundtrack album on Atlantic Records, shown on HBO, parodied in *Mad* and finally developed into a TV series by Lorimar. And all of the money— along with all of the choices—will be left in the hands of Time Warner, Inc.[26]

While the media are often perceived as liberal sources of social change and criticism, like any institution they are not generally in the business of undermining their own basis of power. U.S. book publishers will, on occasion, publish works that are critical of corporate capitalism, for example, but these are rarely promoted on a wide scale. The situation is even more extreme in the mass

---

[25] See Parenti, op. cit.

[26] Phil Rosenthal, "In Spite of What Executives Say, Proposed Media Conglomerate Is Development to Be Feared," *The Hartford Courant*, April 2, 1989, p. G1. Originally published in the *Los Angeles Daily News*.

media, where regular access to the vast majority of the population is virtually never used as a forum for critical analysis of capitalism and its social consequences. Newspapers, magazines, and television and radio stations are all capitalist corporations, and as such are as dedicated as any government to promoting a self-serving ideology.

Unlike the state, however, these corporations control major cultural technology for disseminating ideas and knowledge, giving them the power to shape ideology as much through what they say as what they do not. The mass media, for example, are quick to attribute the problems of socialist countries to socialism itself, with the obvious implication that under capitalism life is much improved. In reporting and analyzing the problems of capitalist countries, however, the media never suggest that capitalism itself might be among the causes, an omission that not only perpetuates a nationalistic blindness but also protects the corporations themselves and leaves the social system in which they thrive relatively free of critical analysis.

One of the most fascinating aspects of the reciprocal relationship between material culture and social life is the way in which some objects, once created, become part of the social environment, to which we may attribute an autonomous existence and influence beyond our control. This is especially evident with the increasing use of computers. We seem to think of computers in the same way that we think of human beings—by attributing blame, for example, as well as intentionality. Many people have expressed in one way or another the fear that computers will "take over our lives" (if they have not already). The problem is that computers are quite limited: however fast they may be, for example, they are at present incapable of the subtleties of linguistic interpretation quite within the reach of the average three-year-old human. Even more important, they certainly do not have the consciousness necessary to will or intention, and therefore cannot want, desire, aspire, or, most certainly, "take over." The day may come when computers will be the chess champions of the world, but it is far less likely that they will ever be able to generate creative insight that flows from the kind of brilliant nonlinear leaps of thought that humans are capable of making.

The social problem lies not in the machine, but in our relationship to the machine and the ways in which we think about that relationship, over which we have an enormous potential for control. The machine, after all, is only a machine; without human purpose and direction, it is just metal and plastic. It is nothing more than we make it to be, and has no more significance than we attribute to it. When we say that a machine is efficient, we are not describing the machine, but its functional place in a human arrangement that values some outcomes more than others. The idea of efficiency is a cultural creation that does not exist outside of human thought. It is our *use* of the machine to accomplish goals we have established in a cultural value system that is efficient, not the machine, and our failure to see the difference has serious consequences.

The problem is that when a cultural element develops, we tend to forget that its social origins lie in our collective life, and by so doing we endow it with an autonomy that it otherwise would not have. In some cases (especially with values, beliefs, and other cultural ideas) we act as though it has always existed or is a feature of all societies. Short of this, we often treat it as a necessity so woven into the fabric of our lives that freedom from it comes only at a considerable cost. If we were to suddenly lose access to electricity and fossil fuels—without which the human race survived quite nicely for millions of years—we would face not only the loss of luxuries such as electronic media, but severe shortages of necessities as well. During the great blizzard of 1898, cities such as New York were paralyzed and the provision of life's necessities became a major challenge; but for those living in rural areas, who had not developed a dependency on energy-intensive technology, it was just another storm—albeit a particularly large one—with some threat to livestock, but otherwise no cause for great alarm.

Paradoxically, in making material culture a part of social environments we tend to fuse with it and externalize it at the same time. We fuse with it in the sense that we depend on and identify with it to such a degree that it is difficult to imagine life without it. However, we externalize it by forgetting that it is nothing more than a physical manifestation of our own collective imagination. The danger of fusion is that we may defend technology or other material culture and refuse to give it up even when its presence and use threaten our best interests; the danger of externalization is that even if we want to change or get rid of technology, we perceive ourselves as being either helpless or not responsible, or both.

In this way we find ourselves feeling and acting as though we are at the mercy of inanimate objects. We also effectively avoid taking collective or individual responsibility for creations that arise from the social life of which our individual lives are a part. Our denial does not protect us from the consequences, however, for as Robert Merton's corollary of W. I. Thomas's famous dictum points out, "if people do *not* define *real* situations as real, they are nevertheless real in their consequences."[27]

Living in the Web

"We live in a web of ideas, a fabric of our own making," wrote the eminent American philosopher Susanne Langer.[28] We do not, however, simply live *in* a web of ideas, for the process of socialization guarantees that each of us is—to some degree—enmeshed in the web itself, which effectively renders the culturally created world invisible to us. And yet, just as the psychological perspective enables us to gain insight into ourselves as individuals by objectifying and standing apart from ourselves to some degree, the sociological perspective enables us to move towards the same kind of reflections of ourselves on a collective level. Our access to a "coherent and steady imagination"[29] allows us to see what is not apparent to our senses, including the abstract threads from which the collective meanings, understandings, and terms of social life are woven.

---

[27] Robert K. Merton, "The Sociology of Social Problems," in Robert K. Merton and Robert Nisbet, eds., *Contemporary Social Problems,* 4th ed. (New York: Harcourt Brace Jovanovich, 1976), p. 22. See also Hubert J. O'Gorman's work on the phenomenon of pluralistic ignorance, which refers to the shared misperception of reality. See, for example, "White and Black Perceptions of Racial Values," *Public Opinion Quarterly* 43 (1979): 48–59, and "The Discovery of Pluralistic Ignorance," *Journal of the History of the Behavioral Sciences* 22 (October 1986): 333–47.

[28] Langer, op. cit., p. 147.

[29] Langer, op. cit., p. 145.

CHAPTER
THREE

——— ◆ ———

The
Structures of
Social Life

.

In 1971 I made my first trip to the small town of San Miguel de Allende, nestled on a mountainside in central Mexico. After two and a half years of graduate school, this was the closest I came to a true vacation—no responsibilities, day after day of long walks, sleep, and taking in the smells, sights, and sounds of the open-air markets, sunbaked adobe, and beautiful gardens.

After several weeks, I had a strange experience. I wanted to know what time it was, and realized that I hadn't been wearing my watch for some time. In trying to figure it out, I could only come up with a rough guess reckoned by the position of the sun. Since I had not been doing anything that required knowing what time it was, I had, understandably, lost my sense of it, which seemed at first an interesting experience. I soon realized, however, that I also did not know what day it was, and even after sitting for awhile could not figure it out. Although I was taken at first by the uniqueness of this, I also felt a bit disconcerted, as if I were a little lost, like coming up out of a subway into a neighborhood that bears no resemblance to your intended destination. In the social sense that I was raised with, "lost" is just what I was.

There are certainly important natural rhythms and cycles in life, but for the most part, knowing the day or the time of day is important only because it allows us to orient ourselves to the expectations of other people. It is one of those cultural creations that gives a sense of structure to social life, resulting in patterns of behavior and interaction that are, to one degree or another, predictable and familiar. I became "time lost" in the mountains of Mexico because I was transplanted from a familiar social environment where the parameters of my life depended on knowing the day and time to one where neither was particularly important. My disconnection from time was in part my disconnection from the structure of my old social environment and in part my failure to adapt to a new one that had less regard for times and dates.[1]

Sociologists have come to appreciate that the concept of structure is crucial to understanding social life because structure gives social systems their sense of form. The structure of a group or society is what results when we take abstract cultural ideas about social life—norms, values, and so on—and form them into actual social relationships through which, in turn, people form and experience themselves as participants. When we move to a radically different environment or lose our jobs or become divorced or widowed, we often feel not just a sense of loss but a sense of being lost. This results from the disruption of our position in the social structure, and a consequent loss of a sense of self in the patterns of expectation and interaction both with others and with groups, communities, and societies.

Structure refers to the relationships that make up social systems and the various distributions that result from them. Relationships consist of patterns of expectation and interaction

---

[1] For more on the sociological significance of time, see R. H. Lauer, *Temporal Man: The Meaning and Uses of Social Time* (New York: Praeger, 1981) and E. Zerubavel, *The Seven-Day Circle: The History and Meaning of the Week* (New York: The Free Press/Macmillan, 1985).

whose participants may consist of everything from individuals to entire nations or collection of nations. In addition to their cultural aspects, these relationships have a variety of structural character-istics, from patterns of communication to the uses of time and the mixture of roles people perform. Both singly and in combination, these characteristics have many different effects on what happens in social systems, and as such need to be understood apart from the intentions of the people who participate in them.

Structure also refers to various kinds of distributions in social systems. As previously noted, the richest one percent of U.S. families owns 66 percent of all business assets while the bottom 90 percent owns only 6 percent—this describes an important part of the socioeconomic structure of this society,[2] as does the fact that the vast majority of presidential cabinet members (including secretar-ies of labor) have upper or corporate class origins.[3] As well, less than 20 percent of working people belong to unions and most people have jobs with low levels of authority, autonomy, security, or control over work conditions, indicating important structural aspects of labor markets and occupational life in capitalist indus-trial societies. Whether we are talking about the distribution of rewards and resources such as wealth, power, and prestige or the distribution of people among different social statuses, these important structural aspects of social systems can tell us much about how they operate and the social consequences they produce.

Statuses
and Roles

For individuals, the most immediate and important structural aspect of a social system are the positions (statuses) they occupy in relationships and the roles they are expected to perform as a result. Each of us occupies many statuses (a status set[4])—from ascribed statuses such as race and gender that we enter at birth, and

---

[2] Democratic Staff of the Joint Economic Committee, *The Concentration of Wealth in the United States* (Washington, DC: Joint Economic Committee, United States Congress, 1986), Table 2.

[3] See G. W. Domhoff, *Who Rules America?* (Englewood Cliffs, NJ: Prentice-Hall, 1967) and B. Mintz, "The President's Cabinet, 1897–1972: A Contribution to the Power Structure Debate," *Insurgent Sociologist* 5 (1975): 131–48.

[4] See Robert K. Merton, *Social Theory and Social Structure*, enlarged ed. (New York: The Free Press, 1968).

acquired statuses such as employee, spouse, and friend, to temporary statuses that come with situations such as being a pedestrian on the street or a customer in a store. To each status there usually are attached not one but several roles (a role set[5]), because each status tends to relate to several others. A psychotherapist, for example, performs roles in relation to a client, a client's family members, and other therapists who might be consulted, as well as insurance companies. If the client is hospitalized, the therapist's role set expands to include relationships with various hospital personnel.

All of these roles are attached to the single status of psychotherapist, and given their multiplicity, it is inevitable that their different expectations will conflict from time to time and produce strain. In many cases strain results because we occupy more than one status, as when therapists are torn between the confidentiality they owe a client who might threaten to kill someone and their obligations as citizens to report such threats to prevent a crime. There are also strains between roles within the role set, as when therapists are called upon by the families of clients (who might also be paying the bills) to reveal confidential information about what clients have done or said during therapy. Strain also can occur when the boundaries that distinguish one status from another become blurred, as when former psychotherapy clients begin friendships with their therapists and both find that the expectations of their former relationship are difficult to distinguish from the expectations attached to their new one. The line that separates emotionally supporting a friend and emotionally supporting a client, for example, can be very difficult to identify. This is a major reason why many professional psychotherapists feel ethically bound to avoid any ties with clients outside of the client-therapist relationship.

In the simplest sense this micro-level of social structure is important because it is through roles that behavior is socially regulated by ideas about how status occupants are expected to appear and behave. Therapists, for example, are not supposed to have sex with their clients, and clients are expected to pay their bills and make reasonable efforts to use the help offered to them. That inappropriate sexual behavior on the part of therapists is becoming increasingly common in the United States

---

[5] Ibid.

(primarily between male therapists and female clients) underscores the fact that a role is simply a set of expectations to which actual behavior does not always conform. It also highlights the fact that each status and its role set exists within a larger social environment that affects how people perform their roles. Thus, in spite of their professional ethical standards and obligations, therapists are not immune to the effects of gender relations and inequality and the forces that lead to a general prevalence of sexual abuse of females in many societies.

Statuses and roles are also important because, by defining the structure of social space, they locate us in relation to other people. We are known to most people not by the personal characteristics that make us unique, but by the content of our status and role sets. At birth we are known only by a handful of statuses such as gender, race, surname, daughter or son, and brother or sister, for there is relatively little else about us to know (or, if there is, it is largely inaccessible to those around us). Thereafter, constructing a social identity is a process of acquiring statuses and learning to think of ourselves in terms of them. As Goffman points out, the roles that accompany each status include a ready-made self that each occupant is expected to identify with, whether the scholarly air of a college professor, the discipline of a professional athlete, or the compassion of a nurse.[6] In this sense, we are known less for what we are in some internal sense than by the images of us contained in shared beliefs about our statuses and roles. In social space we are not "who we are": we are who people think we are, and who they think we are has more to do with social systems than anything else.

One implication of this is that we also tend to know ourselves through role relationships. If we build on the discussion in Chapter 2 of Mead's idea that we discover ourselves through discovering others, it follows that our definition, perception, and evaluation of ourselves is mediated by our status and role sets. In constructing ideas of who we are, we depend in part on how we think other people see us—what Charles Horton Cooley called the "looking-glass self"[7]—and in evaluating ourselves, we either look to others or imagine putting ourselves in their place.

The "others" involved in this process are of two basic types. In

---

[6] Erving Goffman, *Encounters* (Indianapolis, IN: Bobbs-Merrill, 1961).
[7] Charles Horton Cooley, *Life and the Student* (New York: Knopf, 1927).

many cases, we look to specific individuals (what psychiatrist Harry Stack Sullivan called significant others)—from members of our families to casual acquaintances. The second "other," while less specific, is in many ways socially more important. This consists of our perception of how people in general view a social situation and the occupants of different statuses within it (an "other" that Mead aptly dubbed "generalized").[8] Because the ideas attached to statuses are shared cultural ideas, we tend to assume that once our statuses are known to others, they will perceive and evaluate us in particular ways. How they actually perceive us is in many ways less important than how we *think* they perceive us, for it is our perception of them, based on shared beliefs about a common social environment, that we use to construct our reality of how they see us and how, in turn, we see ourselves. In short, the entire process of perceiving and evaluating ourselves and others depends on our perception and knowledge of social structure.

It is through the continuing overlap of our status and role sets with those of others that we are connected to the social world, and each overlap serves to locate, identify, and anchor us in social space. Without them, we do not exist socially, and without a social existence there is not much left of what we know as our human selves. Nothing in this need detract from our sense of dignity except to the extent that dignity is based on an illusion that we are self-made and self-sustaining. It simply means that whoever we are, whether in blind conformity to role expectations or in open rebellion against them, we exist largely through our location and participation in social systems. The most iconoclastic rebels—who claim to reject what binds them to their social environment— define themselves through what they reject, and occupy an existing social status ("rebel") with its own role expectations. Even the most bizarre and outlandish person has a recognizable structural position, as evidenced by the simple inclusion of the category "bizarre" in our language. To extend Susanne Langer's idea, the reality we construct is not simply something human in a cultural sense; it is also profoundly structural.[9]

---

[8] George Herbert Mead, *Mind, Self, and Society* (Chicago: University of Chicago Press, 1934).

[9] Susanne K. Langer, "The Growing Center of Knowledge," In *Philosophical Sketches* (Baltimore: Johns Hopkins Press, 1962), p. 146.

This does not mean we are reducible simply to status and role sets, for just as a group is more than a collection of individuals, so, too, each individual is more than an occupant of a set of structural positions. The lack of uniformity in the socialization process combined with the great variety in the ways individuals respond to the constraints and limitations imposed by systems guarantee a great deal of play and slippage in the fit between individuals and social structures, a lack of fit that makes social life both interesting and dynamic.

Societies and individuals exist through a dynamic interdependence in which, although neither is reducible to the other, it is impossible to have one without the other. Just as it is impossible to have social systems without people, it is impossible to have a person without social systems, even if such systems are no more than what has been internalized in the socially constructed self of a person living alone on a desert island. Even if we accept that there is an existential human self that transcends all social environments, it is a self we can barely experience as such, so mediated is everything we know by the social environment in which we know it.

Social Structure and Individuals

The key sociological proposition that the whole is more than the sum of its parts can be extended to an understanding that the whole exists to some degree independently of particular sets of parts. In other words, although social statuses would not amount to much if *no* one occupied them, they exist independently of being occupied by particular people at any particular time. The U.S. Supreme Court, for example, is an institutional structure for resolving disputes over the interpretation of constitutional rights; as such, it is far more than the nine people who currently act as justices. If they all died in a plane crash tomorrow, the structure of the Court, and its statuses of "associate justice" and "chief justice," would exist as part of the social environment even though unoccupied at the moment.

The existence of social arrangements outside of the individuals who participate in them is particularly important to social institutions. An institution is an enduring set of arrangements organized around one or more activities or goals that are socially valued, from the socialization of children to the dispensation of justice. An institution is a sort of blueprint providing a framework for doing things, and as such, it may be quite distinct from what people actually do. In accordance with our cultural notions of what family life is supposed to be like, for example, most parents do not abuse their children, but many nonetheless do. Similarly, the fact that the police sometimes violate people's civil rights or politicians and judges sometimes take bribes or otherwise violate the public trust are separate from the ideals that define those rights and the object of that trust.

The distinction between social structures and individuals is especially important in highly individualistic societies such as the United States, where we routinely confuse status occupants with the statuses themselves and the consequences of individual behavior with the consequences of social systems. Legal scholars who study the Supreme Court, for example, point out that the political views of new appointees are often a poor indicator of how they will actually vote on Constitutional cases, in large part because "Supreme Court Justice" is a highly constraining status. Although technically free to vote as they please, justices do not in fact feel at all free to do so because, among other factors, the cultural values and norms of the court strongly discourage overturning precedents set by past decisions. The status and its role set are quite distinct from particular status occupants and are often better predictors of behavior.

In this sense, when Napoleon declared "I am the state" to the French Senate in 1814, he made a fundamental sociological error that politicians continue to make today, although in more subtle ways. Voters in their hopes and candidates in their promises and aspirations seem to believe that national leaders have far more ability to alter basic institutional arrangements than in fact they have. New leaders often assume office with a proposed agenda of fundamental changes, but soon come up against the hard reality that social systems are not easily changed. Intentions to overhaul foreign policy, for example, quickly become mired in the realization that the agreements, understandings, and mutual obligations among nations are not only long-standing, but extraordinarily complex; and because they exist between nations and not individuals, they cannot be undone simply by the will of individual officeholders. Presidents and prime ministers may be among the most powerful political officeholders in the world, but office*holders* is what they are, and like every status, the office constrains as much as, if not more than, it empowers.

In a sense this misstates the case, for it is not the status per se that constrains, but the relationship of each status to other statuses. The status of father, for example, exists only in relation to the statuses of daughter, son, and mother, without which it has no meaning or power to constrain. This is true of every status, which means that the focus of attention in structural analysis at the micro level is not the individual status per se, but the role relationship— the nature of the connection among statuses. These relationships can, of course, be quite complex, as they are in bureaucracies, and can also exist between groups or communities or, in the case of foreign policy, among nations. In each case, the key to understanding behavior and events lies in examining the structural characteristics of relationships.[10]

Boundaries and the Effects of Social Structure

Much of human experience (and the problems associated with it)—from grand and public to minute and personal—has its roots in the structural conditions of social life. Social interaction, for example, is affected by the simple fact that every social system and every status within it has boundaries that identify where the system (or status) begins and ends. Boundaries identify who occupies a status (such as female, white, lower-class, or professional) and delineate rules about entering and leaving statuses (such as professional licensing requirements or kinship rules that define who is related to whom and how such connections are made and broken). Boundaries vary both in their permeability (anyone can become a pedestrian by simply walking out onto the sidewalk) and their clarity (everyone knows police officers by their uniforms).

---

[10] There are numerous structural characteristics; only some will be discussed in the pages that follow. They include role, power, prestige, communication, time, sociometric structures, the degree of formality of relationships, and types of social cohesion. For a more thorough and systematic treatment, see Allan G. Johnson, *Human Arrangements: An Introduction to Sociology,* 2nd ed. (San Diego: Harcourt Brace Jovanovich, 1989), Chapter 4.

The problems of defining and maintaining boundaries exist in every social system. We are all aware of the formal boundary problems of groups and nations, from college admission requirements to the issue of illegal aliens, and we may be aware of the uses of boundaries to accomplish racial, ethnic, and class distinctions. But we are less aware of the importance of boundaries in role relationships where the mechanisms are less visible and the criteria less codified. Small talk, for example, serves an important boundary-maintaining function by enabling us to be around other people without opening ourselves to deeper levels of self-exposure and intimacy than we want. When we pass a casual acquaintance on the street, we are caught between two contrary tendencies—to maintain our separateness, privacy, and noninvolvement on the one hand, and on the other to draw comfort from being with people and knowing that we are not alone in the world. Often, the compromise between the two takes the form of the familiar "Hi, how are you?" "Fine, how are you?" exchange that on one level seems false and meaningless. As ritual, however, it is quite meaningful, for otherwise we would have to choose between intimate interaction with each person we encountered or complete isolation and separateness. It reaffirms our connection to collective humanity (which explains why we also may greet complete strangers who catch our eye in passing); this is in some ways far more important to us than even our most highly valued personal relationships. There are no specific ties to individuals that cannot and are not eventually broken in one way or another, if only by death; but the deeper tie to our own social environment and those who collectively share in it roots us in a more enduring way.

Even the simplest situations have to be handled with some skill. If we use up our available small talk too soon in a conversation, for example, we tend to feel embarrassed and awkward, and this also has to do with boundaries. When we see someone walking towards us on the sidewalk, we don't say "Hello" when they are some distance away; we wait until we are just about to pass each other. Acknowledging each other too soon opens our boundaries to the possibility of self-disclosure and contact for a longer period than most available small talk can fill, especially with people we barely know (as occurs when we say hello ten or twenty yards too soon and then feel awkward and embarrassed as we grow nearer and feel the absence of something appropriate to say). This simple example illustrates that although we tend not to be aware of it until it is disrupted, even the most informal social interactions have identifiable structures and understandings that affect their participants.

Many problems at first glance seem to be rooted solely in the personalities of individuals or the inner reaches of human nature, but on closer examination they owe at least part of their existence to the vagaries of social structure. This is nowhere more true than in families, which we experience in such personal terms that we overlook the fact that each family is a social system constrained by larger institutional "blueprints" (as in the "ideal" family) and connected to other institutional arrangements such as the economy, schools, religion, and the legal system. Even psychotherapists increasingly use a systems approach to understand the problems of individuals in families, which includes not only role relationships within the family, but the stresses and strains brought to the family by involvements in the larger world.

Emotional and physical abuse found in families, for example, is often explained in terms of individual character disorders, but this ignores the fact that people who abuse children and spouses are often not terribly unlike the rest of the adult population in most respects. Indeed, probably the best predictors of family violence are more structural than psychological, for such violence is most likely in homes strained by financial hardship and unemployment, or where the distribution of power favors husbands over wives. Violence is also made more likely by the extreme emotional and material interdependence and isolation of the nuclear family structure itself: since it is impossible to satisfy the needs and desires of everyone, tension, frustration, and bitterness are too easily acted out on the nearest target, beyond the view of outsiders who might interfere.[11]

Even if we accept psychological disorder as an explanation of family violence, we still come up against the fact that character disorders not only arise from social relationships but are perpetuated in them as well. It is not at all uncommon for disorders such as alcoholism, borderline personality, and even psychotic conditions such as schizophrenia to become so integrated into the relationships and the dynamics of family life that members will

---

[11]See Murray Straus et al., *Behind Closed Doors* (New York: Anchor, 1980); R. J. Gelles and C. P. Cornell, *Intimate Violence in Families* (Beverly Hills, CA: Sage, 1985); and A. Shupe et al., *Violent Men, Violent Couples: The Dynamics of Domestic Violence* (Lexington, MA: Lexington Books, 1987).

sabotage opportunities for individuals to recover their health because this will disrupt the established and familiar social system and everyone's position in it. The simplest form of sabotage is individual and collective denial that a problem exists—that a husband's violence is not violence at all, but "just the way he is," or "getting carried away when he's drunk," and that getting drunk is something other than alcohol abuse or alcoholism.

Language again shows itself to be of great importance in shaping reality, for once labels such as abuse, violence, and alcoholic are applied, the family can no longer deny what is going on, which brings into the open the threat to the family as a system and the investment that every member has in its continued existence. For this reason, family roles are often used to cover behavior that would otherwise be unacceptable. Parents and others, for example, generally do not define behavior as violent if it is associated with their role as parents. Slapping a disobedient child is far less likely to be perceived as violence than slapping a disobedient employee.[12] In this way, language is a cultural screen obscuring perceptions of a situation's structure as a way of perpetuating the system and, ironically, the kind of behavior that threatens its survival.

On a more conscious level, family systems are protected through secrets kept by selected family members, thereby compartmentalizing knowledge of dysfunctional behavior so that no one knows the entire story. Or secrets may be family-wide to protect the family from interference from the outside. Whether through secrets or denial, some family members may find their individual interests sacrificed to preserve the family as a system. We may be quite aware of the ways in which bureaucrats value the system over the individual and routinely cause pain and suffering as a result; but we are less aware that this can occur in any social system in which individuals feel a deep dependency on its continued existence. That wives stay with husbands who abuse them cannot be explained as a simple manifestation of personality traits, such as masochism, without ignoring the fact that these women believe with good reason that theirs and their children's material security depends on maintaining the family system and its

---

[12] For more on this, see Richard J. Gelles, *The Violent Home* (Beverly Hills, CA: Sage, 1972).

claim on the husband's earnings. The importance of such structural constraints becomes more visible when we look at the effects of women's increased economic independence on the rates of divorce: the more secure women become financially, the more likely they are to leave bad marriages.[13] It also fits well with the observation that divorce rates tend to decline during economic depressions[14] and that divorce often impoverishes mothers and children but actually increases the standard of living of fathers.[15]

The structural characteristics of social systems have effects not only on the level of families and role relationships, but also on the larger level of entire societies. Robert K. Merton, for example, argues that many different forms of deviance can be linked with the distribution of opportunities.[16] In the United States, there is a high cultural value on the accumulation of material possessions. People of all social classes are surrounded by a steady stream of advertising with the underlying message that a successful life includes—if not depends upon—an abundance of possessions.

Although most people in the United States have been socialized to value the accumulation of wealth, the structural distribution of opportunities for achieving this goal is far less equal. We are, in other words, more similar in our wants than our access to the legitimate means for satisfying them. This imbalance creates a strain that people may choose to resolve in deviant ways. People who cannot earn enough money to buy a car might steal one, a response that honors the value of owning a car while violating the norms that define legitimate ways of getting one. Another deviant response is to become a drop-out who lives on the fringes of society and disavows both the value of possessions and the system for acquiring them. Still another is to foment revolution

---

[13] See S. J. South, "Economic Conditions and the Divorce Rate," *Journal of Marriage and the Family*, 47,1 (1985):31–41.

[14] See, for example, P. H. Jacobson, *American Marriage and Divorce* (New York: Rinehart, 1959).

[15] See Lenore Weitzman, *The Divorce Revolution: The Unexpected Social and Economic Consequences of Divorce on Women and Children in America* (New York: The Free Press, 1985).

[16] Merton is one of the deans of American sociology and a prodigious authority on the concept of social structure. See his classic *Social Theory and Social Structure*, enlarged ed. (New York: The Free Press, 1968). See also Lewis A. Coser, ed., *The Idea of Social Structure: Papers in Honor of Robert K. Merton* (New York: Harcourt Brace Jovanovich, 1975).

by arguing that cars and other forms of wealth should be distributed in a different way—according to need, for example, or equally.

In either case, the greater the disparity between the distribution of values and the opportunities for material acquisitions, the higher will be the rate of deviance. This means that the incidence of theft depends less on how much or little people have than on the gap between what they have and what others around them have. If everyone in a community has the same standard of living, they will tend to have values in line with their common condition. But if a community has a poor population at one end and a relatively well-off elite at the other, theft will be more common. This is exactly what researchers have found: levels of burglary and larceny are highest in metropolitan areas that have the highest level of income inequality, regardless of the actual levels of poverty.[17]

Merton's structural approach to deviance is helpful in understanding a common problem in universities—students who cheat. Good grades are highly valued, but the distribution of the legitimate ways of achieving them is as unequal as the distribution of talent, ability, and the time and energy available for studying. If we add to this the common practice of scaling or curving grades so that a certain percentage of each class must get low grades to round out the low end of the curve, the result is a set of competitive structural conditions guaranteed to motivate students to cheat (not to mention sabotaging the work of other students to keep the overall curve as low as possible).

Sociologically, understanding the structure of a social system is less useful for predicting individual responses to it than for predicting and understanding the *patterns* of response of which individual behavior is a part. It is similar in this way to predicting the outcome of coin tosses. If we know that a series of tosses is structured so that heads and tails, are equally likely, we can predict that over the long run the pattern of outcomes will approximate a distribution with a roughly equal number of each. Similarly, if we know the procedure favors heads by a ratio of 2:1, roughly two-thirds of the outcomes should come up heads in the long run.

---

[17] See, for example, D. Jacobs, "Inequality and Economic Crime," *Sociology and Social Research* 66,1 (1981):12–28.

This kind of knowledge, however, has little to do with the outcome of a particular toss: it will be either a head or a tail, not "probably" one or the other. The odds for a head might be 2:1 or 1000:1 and the toss might still result in a tail. So it is with the structure of social systems and the individuals who participate in them. Sociology is less concerned with how a particular individual will actually respond to a particular set of social circumstances than with the patterns of behavior and experience that different social systems tend to produce. Whether a particular student cheats is not of sociological significance; that many do or only a few, or that people in some social categories are more likely to cheat than those in other categories, is.

Role, Power, and Communication Structures

In addition to boundaries, social systems have a variety of structural characteristics that are important both singly and in combination with others. Every family, for example, has a role structure consisting of the mix of statuses and roles that operate in that system. Within a given role structure there is a communication structure with patterns of interaction among members that vary in their frequency and duration. Together, these profoundly affect family life. A great deal of the stress experienced by parents in single-parent families, for example, can be attributed to a role structure truncated by divorce and a resulting communication structure in which all of the parent-child interaction is concentrated on one adult rather than being shared with another. A variation on this is found in compound families formed through remarriages in which children are related to only one of the spouses. Here the family includes two adults, but interaction is still focused primarily on the natural parent, with the result that the stepparent often feels excluded. This is especially evident in what J. L. Moreno called the sociometric structure—the network of ties based not on role relationships but on affection.[18] Until they develop their own place in the family system, stepparents often feel that affection, respect, and loyalty are withheld by stepchildren, and as well, experience the competition that often develops over affection and

---

[18] See J. L. Moreno, "Sociometry and the Cultural Order," *Sociometry* 6 (1943):299–344.

loyalty from the natural parent. Coalitions against the stepparent are for this reason especially likely to form and constitute one of the most difficult long-term challenges for compound families.

Closely related to the role structure is the power structure, grounded primarily in the authority attached to each social status. Social power is one of the most important concepts in sociology and also one of the most problematic because its definition can take strikingly different forms. The standard definition is drawn from Max Weber, who is perhaps best known for his prophetic work on the emergence of bureaucracy as the primary way of organizing social power in industrial societies. From Weber's perspective, power is the ability to control others in spite of opposition.[19] This power rests in the ability to control and dominate, a concept firmly rooted in the organization of most contemporary societies. An increasing number of feminist scholars, however, are challenging the idea that this is the only form that power can take. Spiritual power, for example, the power to create rather than destroy, or the ability to work together in partnership in nonhierarchical social systems are all forms of power that have little connection to dominance and control.[20] Social power, however, has become so deeply associated with the ideas of hierarchy, dominance, and control that most people do not feel powerful unless they are in a position to control people, events, or resources.

We can span some of the gap between these alternatives by defining social power as the potential to have an effect, either on ourselves, others, or our environment. This approach includes not only power as dominance and control over others, but also the ability to create or live free of control by others. As such, it certainly does not encompass all of the forms of power that can occur in human life—like spiritual power—but it does include most forms of power that are relevant to the structure of social relationships.

In addition to roles, communication, and power structures, social systems vary in the types of relationships that bind them together. As distinct from secondary relations that exist to accomplish narrowly defined goals, primary ties rest on affection, are generalized to include most aspects of people's lives, and place

---

[19] See Max Weber, *The Theory of Social and Economic Organization* (New York: Oxford University Press, 1947. Original edition, 1925). See also Dennis Wrong, *Power: Its Forms, Bases, and Uses* (New York: Harper and Row, 1980).

[20] See Marilyn French, *Beyond Power* (New York: Summit, 1985) and Riane Eisler, *The Chalice and the Blade* (New York: Harper and Row, 1987).

the welfare of individuals above the accomplishment of goals.[21] The family is the quintessential example of primary relationships, which explains in large part why it is the source of both our greatest blessings and our most profound troubles. The deep connections and interdependencies of family life are among the few such ties we ever know; but they also create social conditions in which abusive reactions to frustration, disappointment, worry, and stress are most likely to occur. The family is not only Christopher Lasch's "haven in a heartless world," but among the most physically and emotionally dangerous social systems that people encounter in their daily lives.[22]

The risks of family violence are increased by the nuclear family structure. With only one or two adults in each household and with each household existing independently of all others, the potential for observation of and intervention in violent behavior is far lower than in extended families integrated into a larger community. In the United States, where family violence is reaching epidemic proportions, the family unit is widely regarded not as an extension of its community (as is the case in many preindustrial societies) but as the epitome of privacy and insulation from outside control. Only since the 1970s has the idea begun to erode that domestic violence is a "private family affair." In some states, such as Connecticut, police officers no longer have the discretionary authority to decide whether or not to make an arrest in family violence situations; they must intervene. Such laws represent an opening up of the family structure to link it and the welfare of its members with the community.

Although it is analytically useful to think of the separate effects of each structural characteristic of a social system, their interconnections make them best understood as threads of a more complex fabric. It is also important, however, to be aware of the connections through which the structures of different social systems affect one another. One of the most interesting and

---

[21] The concept of primary relations is most closely associated with the early American sociologist Charles Horton Cooley; see his *Social Organization* (New York: Schocken Books, 1962. Original edition, 1909).

[22] Christopher Lasch, *Haven in a Heartless World: The Family Besieged* (New York: Basic Books, 1977). For recent work on family violence, see Richard Gelles and C. P. Cornell, *Intimate Violence in Families* (Beverly Hills, CA: Sage, 1985) and A. Shupe et al., *Violent Men, Violent Couples: The Dynamics of Domestic Violence* (Lexington, MA: Lexington Books, 1987).

compelling examples of these kinds of connections is the relationship between the family and economic institutions.

Family and Economy:
How Systems Affect Each Other

Prior to the industrial revolution and the rise of capitalism, production of goods took place primarily within families. Although family power structures were patriarchal, their role structures were largely centered on women (gynocentric), since women were responsible for rearing children and the production of most goods, including such necessities as cloth, candles, clothing, food, and soap.[23] Women, in short, were subordinate in the power structure but central and indispensable in both the family role structure and society as well. To some degree, the strong interdependence between men and women dampened the effects of the patriarchal structure, for most men needed women too much to take full advantage of their authority as heads of their families.

These family role structures also included an important place for children. Since a large majority of families lived on farms, children were expected to do economically productive work at an early age. When public schooling was introduced on a wide scale in the mid and late nineteenth century, even the school vacation calendar was organized around the need for child labor during the summer growing season. This kind of role structure supported a communication structure with considerable interaction between children and both parents. Since people worked and lived in the same place, fathers were generally in as good a position as mothers to oversee and interact with their children.

The rise of industrialization in the nineteenth century dramatically changed all this in ways that are still felt today. By shifting production from the home to the factory, industrialization made it increasingly difficult for most people to live and work in the same place. This created—for the first time in human history—a dilemma for parents who could not work and take care of children at the same time. As a result, wives stayed at home while

---

[23] See John Demos, *A Little Commonwealth* (New York: Oxford, 1970); John Demos, *Past, Present, and Personal: The Family and the Life Course in American History* (New York: Basic Books, 1986); and Barbara Ehrenreich and Deidre English, *For Her Own Good* (Garden City, NY: Anchor, 1979).

husbands went to work for wages, creating a dramatic shift in family role and communication structures. For the first time, childcare was regarded as a full-time occupation for women along with domestic work that did not involve the production of goods. Interaction with children focused increasingly on mothers, and husbands and wives no longer worked side by side.

At the same time, industrialization steadily supplanted the productive roles of women as more and more goods were manufactured at mass market prices that made it impractical for women to make their own. One by one, the production of goods for home consumption shifted from the home to the factory; the result was a steady shrinking of women's productive role and standing in both the family and society at large.[24]

The shift in productive roles included children as well. As production in the home declined, competition between child and adult workers and concern over the exploitation of children in factories increased, resulting in laws that banned child labor and introduced compulsory schooling. "Adolescence" emerged as a period between childhood and productive adult status and, with it, dramatic shifts in cultural views of young people. As children lost economic value in families, they acquired increasing emotional value, but a dependent emotional attachment to parents was not—and is not—enough to replace the lost portion of their social identities.[25] The participation of all but the youngest children in the productive life of a society has been until now a nearly universal feature of social life. As this standing eroded, what arose in its place was an expanded peer culture formed in isolation from and often in opposition to the surrounding adult culture, a subculture that has become an increasingly serious source of deviant and often violent behavior.[26] Adolescent males, for example, account for more criminal behavior in the United States than any other age group, and the U.S. has the highest rate of teenage pregnancy in the industrialized world. As Margaret Mead argued in her classic study of adolescence in Samoa, such patterns may well reflect

---

[24] For a powerful analysis of the effects of this change on the health of women, see Ehrenreich and English, op. cit.

[25] See Viviana Zelizer's fascinating history of the shifting images of children during this period, *Pricing the Priceless Child: The Changing Social Value of Children* (New York: Basic Books, 1985).

[26] See S. N. Eisenstadt's classic view of age and peer relations, *From Generation to Generation* (New York: The Free Press, 1956).

historical shifts in family and economic role structures that have deprived U.S. adolescents of a secure, meaningful place in their society.[27]

The structure of productive work under industrial capitalism undermined not only the position of women and children, but that of men as well, for by virtually destroying the family as a productive unit, it removed the most important material basis for patriarchal authority. The world was still organized around the idea of male supremacy and masculine values such as dominance, control, and power over others, but the position of individual men within it shifted dramatically. Most men no longer had authority over production, but worked for wages under conditions dictated by others. This meant that men had to find other ways to demonstrate their manhood, including the ability to subordinate women.

In some ways men could do this by controlling the wages they earned, a situation that touches on another important effect of industrial capitalism on family structure. An industrial economy based on wages rather than production within the family allowed people to survive as individuals by earning money in the occupational marketplace. This broke the tight economic interdependence that had bound women, men, and children together, and because men were not held responsible for childcare, they were the first to experience this new potential for independence. Curiously, many people today believe that this model of family life—in which men leave home to provide for the family's material needs—is a human universal rather than an extraordinarily recent development that, as the massive entry of women into the labor market in the late twentieth century suggests, was to be short-lived.

Starting with the entry of married women into the labor force during the two world wars, and continuing with their massive

---

[27] Margaret Mead, *Coming of Age in Samoa* (New York: Modern Library, 1953. Original edition, 1928). Although critics have questioned the scientific validity of Mead's findings about Samoan society, arguing that her observations were unduly subjective, the preponderance of scholarly views supports her conclusions. See Derek Freeman, *Margaret Mead and Samoa: The Making and Unmaking of an Anthropological Myth* (Cambridge, MA: Harvard University Press, 1983); Lowell D. Holmes, *Quest for the Real Samoa: The Mead/Freeman Controversy and Beyond* (South Hadley, MA: Bergin and Garvey, 1986); and G. E. Marcus, "One Man's Mead," *New York Times Book Review*, March 27, 1983, p. 3.

influx in the decades that followed, women now are completing a transformation of family role structures that began with men more than a century ago. Far from representing a radical departure from traditional family life, working wives are part of a long-term adjustment of family role structures to an industrial world in which, as in preindustrial societies, most adults must participate in production for families to meet their needs. As with the exit of men from the home during the Industrial Revolution, this latest shift has created strains in family structures, most notably with childcare. This is less a result of the women's movement than of an historical tension between economic and family structures, a tension that was first eased by the confinement of women to their homes and their economic dependence on their husbands. With women now completing the transition by moving into the occupational marketplace, they are no longer available to resolve this tension, with the result that there is a growing childcare crisis in the United States.

The ability of large numbers of adults to meet their own needs by themselves rather than as part of a family was unheard of before industrialization, and it may have forever changed the relationships between women, men, and children in industrial societies. In the U.S., more people are now living in one-person households than ever before, and the percentages of men and women in their late twenties who have never married have increased dramatically, so that nonfamily households are growing in number at a faster rate than families. These structural trends will, inevitably, produce strains of their own whose effects will be felt not only in family life, but in the structure of the economy as well.

The Relationship Between Culture and Social Structure

Like culture, social structure is an analytic concept useful for identifying and studying different aspects of social life. Although it is possible to think of structure separately from other factors such as culture, it is of course always connected to them and does not exist otherwise. The use of such concepts in sociology, as with every discipline, is similar to studying the human nervous system in one part of a human anatomy course and the circulatory system in another. It makes it easier to think about anatomy if we make these distinctions, even though they actually occur as parts of a whole. There is, in short, no such thing as structure without culture, just as there is no such thing as a human nervous system without a circulatory system—except, perhaps, in the human imagination where everything—including such intellectual distinctions—is possible.

The close relationship between structure and culture means there is much to learn by paying attention to the ways in which they are bound up with each other. Racial prejudice, for example, is a cultural attitude that rests on a variety of negative stereotypes about the subjects of the prejudice and positive stereotypes about those who hold it. Prejudice would not be nearly the problem it is if not for its relation to various structural features of society, including school and neighborhood segregation, inequalities of political power, treatment in the legal system, occupational opportunity, income, wealth, health care, and a wide variety of other factors that affect the quality of life. At the very least, prejudice functions as an ideological underpinning for racial inequality and injustice, and as such is a major cultural factor in the perpetuation of major structural aspects of social systems.

It is less clear that prejudice causes inequality since one might also argue that it arises after or along with the development of inequality as a form of ideological rationalization. This implies that the removal of racial prejudice from a culture will be resisted not simply because it would involve giving up habitual ways of thinking and feeling, but also because it would undermine a complex set of structural arrangements that depend on it for support. If most African-Americans, for example, were not confined largely to the lower and working classes, they would compete with the middle class for jobs and would no longer be available to capitalist enterprises as a source of relatively cheap labor. It also follows that even if it were possible to eradicate prejudice, structural inequality would still have to be dealt with. Since the structures in which racial inequality is imbedded are far more complex than racism as a cultural attitude, it is not surprising that we pay more attention to racism than to inequality and that we tend to misinterpret a decline in the overt expressions of racism as an indicator that inequality is no longer a major problem.

There is yet another connection between cultural racism and social structure in the process of eradicating the former through changes in the latter. As a set of stereotypes, racism depends on real or imagined differences that are distorted and exaggerated to benefit one social category at the expense of another. Such beliefs are generalized to all members of the target category and are usually held to be inherent—they are inferior simply because they belong to that category. The most effective way to undermine prejudice is to provide disconfirming evidence by exposure to actual members of the target category. In the case of race, schools and neighborhoods in the U.S. are highly segregated—more than 80 percent of the African-American population would have to change residence in order to bring about racially balanced neighborhoods in which the percentage of each racial category matched the corresponding percentages for the nation as a whole.[28]

A high degree of racial isolation and separation makes it relatively easy to maintain racial stereotypes. If, however, we change the structure of race relations by increasing the frequency of interaction, we create opportunities for different races to experience one another directly rather than through cultural stereotypes. The degree to which such opportunities will decrease prejudice, however, depends on other structural changes. Research shows that interaction is most likely to reduce prejudice not simply when there is a lot of interaction, but when it takes place in relationships in which people occupy similar statuses and depend on one another to accomplish common goals.[29] It therefore should come as no surprise that desegregation efforts have been more successful in the military and team sports than other areas, nor should it surprise us that integration in housing and schools increases the frequency of interracial friendships and reduces stereotyping.

Social systems are made up of countless such interrelationships that reinforce and affect one another: a shift in cultural values, for example, may prompt a shift in the structural distribution of wealth or power, or a change in structure of relationships

---

[28] See Reynolds Farley and Walter R. Allen, *The Color Line and the Quality of Life in America* (New York: Russell Sage Foundation, 1987).

[29] For a review of the many studies that show the effects of increased interaction on prejudice, see N. Miller and M. B. Brewer, eds., *Groups in Contact: The Psychology of Desegregation* (New York: Academic Press, 1984). See also Gordon W. Allport's classic work on prejudice, *The Nature of Prejudice* (Garden City, NY: Doubleday/ Anchor, 1954).

may bring about a shift in cultural beliefs and attitudes. In similar ways, changes in one element of social structure will effect changes in others. When soldiers bypass the chain of command and express grievances to officers several levels above their immediate commanders, they are changing the communication structure in ways that threaten to destabilize both the power and role structures, which is why such interactions are generally prohibited by military norms.

Although social systems are held together largely because their cultural and structural elements are mutually reinforcing, their complexity produces contradictions that promote conflict and change. Racial prejudice and inequality of opportunity, and the unequal outcomes they underlie would undergo far less pressure for change than they do were they not in conflict with other cultural ideas, including deeply held values about equal opportunity, fairness, freedom, and distributive justice. (That they exist in the first place and endure depends primarily on belief systems— which define whites as superior human beings, for example, or define class systems as the outcome of fair and open competition— that insulate them from the application of values they contradict in reality). As Swedish sociologist Gunnar Myrdal pointed out in his classic analysis of race in the United States, this built-in contradiction creates dilemmas whose strain towards resolution makes change inevitable.[30]

Marx based much of his analysis of capitalism and social change on the idea of built-in structural contradictions that lead, he believed, to predictable patterns of change.[31] At the heart of capitalism, for example, are a set of relationships between the capitalist class that owns and manages capital and those who work in return for wages. Capitalists succeed to the degree they are able to keep a portion of the wealth produced by workers; workers, on the other hand, succeed by holding onto as much of the value of what they produce as they can. In Marx's view, the structure of these relationships in itself constitutes a structural contradiction

---

[30] Gunnar Myrdal, *An American Dilemma* (New York: Harper and Row, 1945).

[31] Marx and the conflict perspective have no monopoly on this insight. See, for example, Robert K. Merton, "Discrimination and the American Creed," in *Sociological Ambivalence* (New York: The Free Press, 1976). See also Lewis M. Coser, *The Functions of Social Conflict* (Glencoe, IL: The Free Press, 1956) and *Continuities in the Study of Social Conflict* (New York: The Free Press, 1967).

that is bound to produce conflict since neither class can pursue its own interests except at the expense of the other.[32]

An obvious way to reduce this potential for conflict is to change the structural conditions that promote it, but this requires a change in the fundamental relationships among workers, capitalists, and the means of production, which would also threaten to remove the major basis of power and privilege for the capitalist class. Since the capitalist class constitutes an elite with considerable power across the institutional spectrum of industrial societies, the usual alternative is to keep the system intact by introducing stabilizing relationships, most notably through the intervention of the state. Earlier in this century, when the labor union movement met staunch and often violent opposition from employers, the state was not above the use of armed force, usually to protect the private property rights of the owners of capital.[33] Today, through its relationships with both capitalists and workers, the state mitigates the negative consequences of capitalism to workers by a variety of programs and policies. Unemployment compensation, social security, welfare and medical benefits, low-interest mortgages and college loans, occupational safety regulations, and laws forbidding unfair labor practices—all of these are benefits made necessary to a considerable degree by the normal functioning of the capitalist system.

This kind of counterbalancing stabilizes and perpetuates the status quo in social systems large and small, especially when the contradictions and strains are produced by fundamental cultural or structural features that are not easily changed. To take another social system as an example, it is not unusual for married couples experiencing serious strains in their relationship to have a child as an attempt to bring them closer together. There are also patterns in

---

[32] See Karl Marx, *Capital: A Critical Analysis of Capitalist Production* (New York: International Publishers, 1967. Original edition, 1867), and Karl Marx and Freidrich Engels, *The German Ideology* (New York: International Publishers, 1970. Original edition, 1846). For an insightful and extremely clear analysis of the connections between social problems and the contradictions of capitalism, see Joan Smith, *Social Issues and the Social Order: The Contradictions of Capitalism* (Boston, MA: Little, Brown 1981).

[33] See, for example, L. J. Griffin et al., "Capitalism and Labor Organization," *American Sociological Review* 51,2 (1986):147–67, and N. I. Painter, *Standing at Armageddon: The United States, 1877–1919* (New York: W. W. Norton and Company, 1987).

which spouses draw their children into their dysfunctional relationship, often at considerable risk to the child's well-being. In spite of its costs, this kind of triangulation may be tolerated for years to preserve the marital tie. An alternative is to seek couples therapy. In each case—capitalist production and marriage—structural strain in one part of the social system leads to structural modifications that can have a variety of consequences. Particularly in the case of psychotherapy, responses to strain can bring about radical cultural and structural change within the family system. As couples examine the cultural underpinnings of their marriage, they may undergo deep changes in their feelings, beliefs, values, and expectations, with the eventual structural effect of increasing the cohesion of their marriage.

A more drastic outcome, of course, is to dismantle the system altogether through divorce. As anyone who has experienced a divorce knows, however (especially when children are involved), a new and more complex family system emerges that has more structural potential for conflict than the one it replaces. Although divorce may decrease strain by separating parents whose personalities clash, the splitting of households makes it more likely that parents will try to undermine each other's authority or children will form coalitions with one parent against the other. In addition to the strains of single-parent families, when parents remarry and form compound families, the structure of family relations can become extraordinarily complex (given their small size) as children acquire multiple sets of kin and often feel torn between absent parents and their live-in surrogates.

Systems Within Systems

While it is important to understand the complex structure of a social system such as a family, it is equally important to be aware that each system is related to other systems at many different levels of analysis, that each whole is not only more than the sum of its parts, but is itself usually a part of a larger whole. If we want to understand something like stress in the modern family, the sociological approach only begins with families themselves as social systems. The difficulty that most families now experience—in making ends meet, buying a home, sending children to college, securing affordable health care, as well as the childcare problems resulting from the fact that a majority of families once again depend on the economic productivity of both parents—cannot be understood solely in terms of family characteristics such as role structures, attitudes about child care, or education levels and occupational training. We also have to understand how forces beyond the family isolate family units from the support of their communities. We have to understand how changes in economic institutions—most particularly the development of industrial capitalism in the last two centuries—have made it necessary for people to meet their needs through participation in an impersonal market that requires them to live and work in different places.

Just as families are embedded in communities and communities are embedded in societies, so too are societies embedded in a world of societies whose relationships with one another affect everything from international diplomacy to the stresses of family life. The anxieties and insecurities of workers in the U.S., for example, are deeply connected to a world economy dominated by a competitive ethic that all too readily sacrifices the needs of workers to the pursuit of profit. When U.S. corporations lay off workers in order to make themselves more competitive—and profitable—in relation to foreign corporations, or when the decline in the buying power of wages makes it necessary for both wives and husbands to work outside the home, or when the strain of financial insecurity contributes to increases in family violence, we are seeing effects on family life whose sources range from the dynamics of family role, communication, and power structures to corporations and communities to international politics and the world economy.

In thinking sociologically, it is important to develop the ability to move with some ease among these different levels of analysis and see how social systems are nested in sets of relationships with other systems. It is only in this way that we can understand not only what goes on within a particular system, but why systems such as the family or economy differ from one society to another and why they change historically.

There is another kind of context, however, that has nothing to do with culture and social structure. It is a physical context whose characteristics and processes profoundly affect what goes on in social systems. For this we must turn to a consideration of human ecology and population.

CHAPTER
FOUR

— ◆ —

Population
and Ecology

— ◆ —

People, Places,
and Things

Although culture and social structure are at the heart of the sociological view of the world, we cannot ignore the fact that social systems exist in relation to a physical environment and cannot function without a supply of people whose material needs are met in relation to that environment. In short, culture and social structure are little more than abstractions without the concrete realities of production and reproduction.

Marx took this observation to its extreme, arguing that the mode of production—the physical means and social relationships through which societies use the environment to produce goods— is the substructure upon which all other aspects of social life are built. Religion, politics, law, medicine, the arts, marriage and the family, popular culture, science, and education, Marx believed, ultimately reflect the mode of production through which societies transform nature in order to survive.[1]

We do not have to embrace this extreme view to realize we cannot fully understand groups and societies without accounting for their relation to their environment. Whether we study the effects of climate and topography on the development of social inequality or institutions such as the state, or the ways family interaction patterns are affected by whether or not each member has a private bedroom, physical and social arrangements are related in complex and important ways. By themselves, culture and social structure and their effects can be understood fully only by including their physical parameters—the spaces in which they exist and the human beings who participate in them.

Ecosystems and Social Systems

In a general sense, ecology is the study of ecosystems, which consist of populations of species that meet their needs and (for humans) wants through relationships to one another and the physical environment they share. The delineation of an ecosystem is somewhat arbitrary and is done solely for analytic purposes. A pond, for example, can be studied as an ecosystem, but what happens to it as a system and to the creatures that inhabit it clearly depends on external forces such as the emission of industrial pollutants perhaps thousands of miles away that create acid rain. Similarly, a city can be studied as an ecosystem, so long as we do not forget the larger context in which it exists. Deciding what constitutes an ecosystem depends less on absolute boundaries than on the scale and complexity of the relationships we are interested in, which can range from a single drop of water to the entire earth and its atmosphere (or, theoretically at least to the solar system and beyond).

The idea of an ecosystem is sociologically useful in several ways. For one, culture and social structure sometimes can be interpreted as collective adaptations and responses to physical

---

[1] It is for this reason that "materialism" is so closely associated with Marxist thought. See Tom Bottomore, ed., *A Dictionary of Marxist Thought* (New York: Basil Blackwell, 1983), pp. 324–29.

environments.[2] In his well-known analysis of "cultural material-ism," for example, anthropologist Marvin Harris argues that the Hindu religious prohibition from eating beef—which puzzles many Westerners trying to understand the chronic and devastating hunger in India—is in fact a rational cultural response to ecological conditions.[3]

The cow is a useful animal in an agricultural economy based primarily on the cultivation of rice. Unlike the horse, the cow has a cloven hoof that does not get stuck by suction in muddy rice fields. In addition, cow dung has a variety of uses, from fertilizer to fuel and making bricks. Its practical uses, however, are not enough to justify making the cow a sacred animal. The key to this is India's climate, which includes periodic droughts of disastrous proportions. During these droughts and the consequent famines, farm families who eat their cattle will meet short-run needs but only by destroying their future ability to cultivate crops when the rains return, so the cows must be protected. Harris argues that religious belief is one of the few social factors powerful enough to overcome such self-destructive tendencies; consequently, the cow is granted sacred status. Thus, while this element of Hindu religion may seem arbitrary and a foolish waste of readily available protein to beef-eating Westerners, it is in fact ecologically sound. Indeed, one can argue that the U.S. practice of cultivating millions of acres to feed beef cattle is a highly wasteful and inefficient indulgence made possible by the vast surpluses of grain the United States produces. Under different climatic conditions, the high cultural value placed on eating meat might change dramatically.

Harris and other cultural materialists argue that physical conditions have a causal effect on the development of culture and social structure. But the concept of an ecosystem is also important because it incorporates the ideas of reciprocal and multiple causation—through the ecosystem, each part has the potential to affect and be affected by all the others. Each species occupies a niche, consisting of its functional interrelationships with other

---

[2] For an extended sociological treatment of this theme that is full of examples, see Gerhard Lenski and Jean Lenski, *Human Societies*, 5th ed. (New York: McGraw-Hill, 1987). See also the popular and provocative work of anthropologist Marvin Harris, *Cows, Pigs, Wars, and Witches* (New York: Random House, 1974), *Cannibals and Kings* (New York: Random House, 1977), and *Cultural Materialism* (New York: Random House, 1979).

[3] See Harris, 1974, op. cit.

species and the physical environment. Bird and insect populations, for example, exist in a balanced relationship, and the fate of each depends on the other, as well as other participants in the system. If a change in the ecosystem—such as the introduction by humans of pollutants in the food chain—shrinks the bird population, the insect population can be expected to increase accordingly. As the insect population outgrows its food supply, its numbers will then die back and, barring other changes, the system will then stabilize with a new balance between the different populations. Every change in an ecosystem, then, has the potential to affect every other aspect of the system in nonlinear and often unpredictable ways.

For most species, niches are relatively simple: each species occupies a certain position in the food chain, for example, and can alter the environment in subtle ways by building habitats, and so on. Human populations, however, occupy extraordinarily complex niches because we enter ecosystems at many different points and produce many different effects. We consume an enormous variety of plant and animal life, for example, and our ability to alter the shape of the land, to build structures, to burn forests, to introduce toxic substances, and, most recently, to alter both plant and animal genetic structures creates the potential for effects so complex that it is impossible to predict more than a minuscule proportion of them. While most other species are narrow ecological specialists who can change their niches only through genetic mutation, humans are generalists largely because we can use culture in the form of technology to rapidly alter our niches. Although Westerners— white men in particular—like to think that we use these abilities to rule or manage the earth, it is more realistic to say that we have the greatest potential to alter the balance in ecosystems, but the effects we produce are usually apparent to us only after the fact. This means that we have both the greatest potential to do damage and that we are probably the only ones with the potential to avoid it: only we can save us from ourselves.

The common perception that the environment is in danger of being damaged and destroyed, however, raises an issue about the nature of ecosystems and how they change, as well as prevailing cultural views of them. Words such as damage, destruction, and saving have meaning only in human value systems. When we say the environment is being destroyed, we are saying that certain culturally valued states in nature are threatened. But these values are ours, since ecosystems as systems have no inherent values. In nature there is no greater value placed on a human community than on a lake full of algae. Indeed, for the vast majority of the earth's 4.6 billion years, ecosystems consisted largely of what humans consider lower life forms, including an initial period of some 2.6 billion years with no life at all and another billion years with nothing more than bacteria and algae. Single-celled protozoa appeared only 800 million years ago, and multicelled blue-green algae colonies developed only 600 million years ago. What we think of as plants are only 500 million years old, and mammals are only 200 million years old.[4] In short, the earth took the vast majority of its existence to develop from a state of lifelessness to a swamp, and has only in the most recent past—a mere twinkling of an eye in relative terms—taken the form so many of us identify as nature.

If we take the long view, ecosystems cannot be damaged or destroyed; they simply change in their physical characteristics, the mix of life forms that inhabit them (which may or may not include humans and what they value), and the network of functional relationships through which life goes on. In some ways our alarm over the effects we have on ecosystems arises from the same species arrogance as the damage many of us so abhor: we assume that cultural value systems are inherent and govern the rest of the natural world, that the value we place on various aspects of nature are universal, shared not only across human cultures, but across species of life and some 4 to 5 billion years of earth history, almost all of which did not include human beings. Unwittingly, those who would save the environment share with those who would destroy it what might be called species centrism, a blindness to the effects of culture as culture. This does not mean that we should not act on cultural values, but it does suggest that people on both sides of environmental issues have more in common than they think and face similar challenges in self-understanding. Whenever we forget the cultural basis for values and assume that they transcend the limited range of human experience and perception, we risk arrogating to ourselves an authority and sense of righteousness that can be as dangerous as it is benevolent.

Although we are more aware these days of the effects that humans have on ecosystems, it is equally important to know the ways ecosystems limit and effect societies. For example, one

---

[4] See Helena Curtis, *Invitation to Biology*, 4th ed. (New York: Worth, 1985).

response to the threats environmental pollution poses to cultural values about the natural world and to the quality of human life has been to challenge the deep-seated value placed on the right to acquire and own property and, as part of ownership, do what we want with it. This extends all the way from personal consumption habits to the cultural underpinnings of corporate capitalism and state socialism. Recent proposed ordinances in southern California sought to ban the use of such mundane personal items as gasoline-powered lawn mowers and backyard barbecues that use charcoal starter fluid. In Vermont, legislation would bar the sale of new cars that use ozone-damaging chemicals in their air conditioners. Some states and communities are mandating recycling and banning the use of nonbiodegradable containers such as styrofoam containers used to package meat in supermarkets and meals in fast-food restaurants. Across the country corporations are being challenged about polluting in the pursuit of competitive advantage and profit.

From public outrage over the giant Exxon oil spill off the coast of Alaska in 1989 and legal pressure on midwestern power companies to clean up coal-burning emissions that cause acid rain in the northeastern U.S. and Canada, to lawsuits against companies that dump toxic wastes in waterways and landfills, the environmental movement is doing more than respond to changes in the ecosystem. In effect if not in intent, it also raises a fundamental challenge to the primacy of cultural values placed on economic growth, competitiveness, profit, and property rights over those placed on the quality of community life and an unspoiled environment. It also challenges the deeply-held value that people have the right to acquire and use property—from barbecues to automobiles to land—without interference from the community or accountability to community interests. As such, the environmental movement, a social response to a changing ecosystem, can play a part in bringing about profound cultural and structural change.

The Mode of Production

The niches that human societies occupy in ecosystems have many different characteristics, but from a sociological perspective, perhaps the most important is the mode of production, the way we use technology and organize production as a social activity. Gatherer-hunter[5] societies, for example, rely on very simple technology and produce none of their own food; horticultural societies grow small gardens and agricultural societies use the plow to cultivate large fields. Industrial societies differ from the others by focusing less on agriculture than on the fabrication of finished goods from raw materials. In addition to these four basic types, there are several others, including fishing and herding societies, and postindustrial societies, the latter concerned less with production than with the delivery of services.

The mode of production goes a long way towards defining the ecological niche occupied by a society and has far-reaching and complex effects on the physical environment, and the cultural and structural nature of the society itself, the latter being generally of most interest to sociologists. There are, for example, systematic differences in religious organization and belief according to the mode of production. In comparison with agricultural societies, gatherer-hunter and horticultural societies are far less likely to believe in the existence of a supreme creator, especially one who takes an active interest in human affairs and morality. Herding societies are the most likely to believe in an active creator concerned with human morality, perhaps because they envision a deity that watches over them in the same way that they watch over their flocks. Horticultural societies are the most likely to include ancestor worship, because the increased permanence of their settlements makes them feel more connected to the place where ancestors are buried, and they do not have the theistic religions associated with agricultural societies.[6]

Several patterns suggest connections between the mode of production and the way life is viewed in different societies. Gatherer-hunter societies, for example, are more likely than horticultural societies to stress self-reliance rather than obedience in child-rearing. They are also much more likely than either horticultural or agricultural societies to have games that involve

---

[5] Although common usage reverses the order—hunter-gatherer—this reflects the misperception that hunting was the predominant source of food in these societies, which has been corrected by more recent archeological and anthropological work.
[6] See Lenski and Lenski, op. cit., pp. 100, 161.

chance and much less likely to have games that involve strategy. Both of these differences may reflect the uncertainty inherent in the gatherer-hunter mode of production and a heightened sense of their inability to control their surroundings.[7]

In no area of social life is the connection with the mode of production more pervasive and, perhaps, more important than in the phenomena of social inequality and the institutionalization of power. Recent feminist analysis, for example, argues that herding societies may have been the first to elevate the ideas of dominance and control over territory and people to the level of central organizing principles of social systems.[8] Their nomadic way of life included a regular need to occupy new territory, and through the breeding of animals, they may have been the first to discover the facts of human reproduction, which in turn may have undermined the reverence and awe felt towards women as the creators of life. This discovery also might have changed the relationship between human communities and the nonhuman natural world, with consequences for human societies as well. To raise animals and then kill them, people must avoid feeling attached to the animals and, by extension, to the natural world of which they and humans are a part. This kind of disconnection from and objectification of the nonhuman world may have formed the basis for disconnection, objectification, and dominance relations among humans as well. As a result, these societies may have been the source of patriarchy and the institutionalization of dominance relations both within and among societies that go with it.

As we cross the range from gatherer-hunter to industrial societies, there is a steady increase in private ownership of land, the existence of class systems, the likelihood of a state, the power of political leaders, and the use of warfare.[9] Much of the ecological basis for social stratification rests on the ability to produce surplus wealth, which forms the basis for power.[10] Production of a surplus also supports an increasingly complex division of labor because as

---

[7] Lenski and Lenski, op. cit., pp. 133, 136.
[8] See Riane Eisler, *The Chalice and the Blade* (New York: Harper and Row, 1987) and Elizabeth Fisher, *Woman's Creation: Sexual Evolution and the Shaping of Society* (New York: McGraw-Hill, 1979.)
[9] Lenski and Lenski, op. cit., pp. 128, 101, 126, and 164.
[10] For an extended and important discussion of this argument, see Gerhard Lenski, *Power and Privilege* (New York: McGraw-Hill, 1966).

a shrinking portion of the population must be engaged in productive work, a larger portion can perform specialized functions, including not only arts, crafts, and various services, but also the support functions for power and privilege, from servants to police and soldiers to tax collectors and political officials. While none of this makes inequality inevitable, together they create the underlying conditions that make it possible. Gatherer-hunter societies, for example, simply have no material basis for a stratification system based on anything other than prestige. Since their populations must move to more abundant surroundings on a regular basis, even if they could accumulate a surplus it would make little sense to accumulate possessions to be carried over considerable distances.

How could the mode of production be related to so many different aspects of social environments? To some degree, we can rely on Marx's basic observation that since productive work lies at the heart of social life, the way it is organized will have widespread and complex effects. But in many cases it is not the mode of production per se that produces social effects. Many are felt indirectly through two major direct consequences of the mode of production—the ability to produce a surplus and the process of population growth and urbanization that generally goes along with it. The mass media, bureaucracy, formal schooling, stratification, complex divisions of labor, the development of political institutions such as the state and, in modern industrial societies, mass party politics, all are closely connected to urbanization—which is to say, large concentrations of population freed from the necessity of growing food—and the productive capacity that makes it possible. Indeed, the phenomenal increase in productivity that accompanied the industrial revolution in the eighteenth and nineteenth centuries could not have happened without the growing concentration of workers in urban areas that accompanied it.

The mode of production is, in many cases, important primarily because it creates conditions in which various developments such as bureaucracy are most likely to occur. It is not a rigid relationship, however, in which a particular mode of production such as industry is a necessary and sufficient condition for a particular social arrangement. Bureaucracy, for example, is a widely recognized aspect of industrialization, but it existed in preindustrial societies such as China for centuries. And although urbanization has progressed the furthest in industrial societies, it is now developing rapidly in countries such as India, Mexico, and Egypt in the absence of major industrial development and, as a consequence, it is greatly exacerbating problems of poverty and homelessness.[11]

Birth, Death, Migration:
Population and Social Systems

A population's position in an ecosystem depends not only on its mode of production, but also on its size, spatial distribution, and rate of growth. This is true regardless of the size of a social system, since each system exists only through the people who participate in it and thus depends on some combination of reproduction and recruitment.

In this sense there are population issues not only for communities, nations, and regions of the world, but also on the much smaller level for groups and organizations such as schools, professions, and religions.[12] The post-World War II "baby boom," for example, played a part in the rapid increase in the college population during the 1960s and a corresponding expansion of college faculties. As the college-age population shrank with the decline and eventual end of the baby boom in the mid-1960s, however, enrollments contracted severely; by the 1980s all but the most prestigious universities had to resort to aggressive advertising campaigns to bolster sagging enrollments, and many smaller colleges went out of business altogether.

Ironically, at the same time, faculties that had expanded so quickly during the 1950s and 1960s virtually stopped growing, and the resulting long-term decline in college teaching opportunities (especially for promotion to senior, tenured ranks) discouraged college graduates from investing the time and money to earn advanced degrees necessary for college teaching. In the long run—which is the time frame involved with most population-based changes—even though the college-age population is expected to increase during the late 1990s, many universities worry that there will then be a shortage of professors to teach them.

---

[11] This phenomenon has come to be known as overurbanization, reflecting the imbalance between urban population growth and the productive capacity necessary to support it.

[12] For this reason, most demographers are closely associated with sociology.

The size and growth of a social system's population depends on a relatively simple process of addition and subtraction—the births, deaths, in-migration, and out-migration whose rates determine not only overall population size and growth, but also key characteristics such as age structure. In a system like a school or business, births and deaths play a minor role in population growth, which is mostly the net result of patterns of in- and out-migration. In communities and societies, of course, birth and death rates play a crucial part in expanding or shrinking the population.

The rate of natural increase is calculated as the birth rate minus the death rate, with both rates calculated as the number of births or deaths per 1,000 people in the population. In the late 1980s, estimated rates of natural increase in the world varied from highs of 3.8 percent in Kenya and Zambia, and 4.3 percent in Gaza to slightly negative rates of increase in Hungary and Germany.[13] Although rates of natural increase may seem like small numbers, the laws of compound interest quickly belie that notion. A population whose rate of natural increase is just 2.0 percent, for example, will double in 35 years and quadruple in 70—roughly the average human lifespan.[14] This means that, ignoring migration, the population of Kenya could be expected to double in only 18 years, and the world population—now growing at a rate of 1.8 percent—could double in 39 years from roughly 5 billion to some 10 billion. Such projections assume, of course, that the rate of natural increase will remain stable, which, if past experience is any guide, is not a terribly reliable assumption.[15] The numbers do provide, however, a good indication of the consequences of different levels of sustained growth.

In many parts of the world—especially those with low rates of

---

[13] The quality of data on births and deaths is always subject to question, especially in nonindustrial societies that typically have poorly-developed registration systems. The best sources of world demographic data are the United Nations (especially their annual *Demographic Yearbook*) and the Population Reference Bureau, 777 Fourteenth Street, Washington, DC 20005).

[14] One can get a rough approximation in figuring doubling times by dividing the number 70 by the rate of increase expressed as a percentage—as in 70/3.5 = 20 years.

[15] Demographers are always quick to point out the important distinction between a projection and a prediction. Although the former is what demographers typically provide, regrettably, the latter is what the public typically makes of it.

natural increase—the effects of migration are an increasingly important part of overall population growth. In the United States, for example, net migration (immigration minus emigration) accounted for just 12 percent of population growth in 1950, but by 1988, when the rate of natural increase had been cut in half, it amounted to 28 percent.[16] Illegal immigration into the United States has grown so rapidly that no one really knows just how many people cross the border each year. At current rates, it is estimated that Spanish-speaking people will make up a majority of California's population by the year 2000.[17] In many parts of Europe, competition between foreign-born and native workers has become so extreme that there have been social movements calling for the expulsion of immigrant workers in Britain, France, and Germany.

Births, deaths, migration, and the patterns of population growth and distribution that result are sociologically important because they are social processes that can be understood as such and have profound effects on both ecosystems and social systems. Birth rates, for example, are affected by cultural and structural factors. They are higher in societies in which women have little education or involvement in the nondomestic labor force, and where male children are valued more highly than females. Although this last difference is found in many societies, it varies considerably in its intensity—where males are highly preferred, wives often bear many children to ensure having a male. Fertility is also higher in societies that value early and universal marriage and early, frequent childbearing—the latter is common in poor, agricultural societies where children play a productive role. In industrial societies, on the other hand, children are economically less productive and are more likely a financial liability than an asset. Not only are there high direct costs of raising children in such societies—especially when higher education is included—but there are also substantial indirect costs incurred when women forego income to stay home and care for children or pay for professional child care.

Economic development is perhaps the most widely explored factor in the explanation of fertility trends and differentials,

---

[16] U.S. Census Bureau, *Statistical Abstract of the United States, 1990* (Washington, DC: U.S. Government Printing Office, 1990), Table 16.
[17] *New York Times*, June 30, 1986.

especially in relation to what is known as the theory of demographic transition. Demographic transition theory attempts to explain the historical pattern of population growth that characterized the now-developed industrial nations during the late eighteenth, nineteenth, and early twentieth centuries. The transition took place in three stages. During the first stage both birth and death rates were high and rates of natural increase were low and stable (a condition that, over the long run, probably describes a great portion of human history). In the second stage, death rates fell as the result of advances in public health and sanitation and improvements in transportation and distribution of food to large populations. As a result, rates of natural increases rose sharply and populations in Europe and the United States grew rapidly.

It is the third stage that is most relevant here, for as societies became more urban and industrial, birth rates fell, resulting in a steady decline in natural increase over the last century or so as birth rates caught up with declining death rates. Historical demographers generally believe that a combination of rising expectations in times of impending economic prosperity and the declining economic value of children motivated couples to limit fertility. Indeed, the motivation must have been strong since most of this remarkable fertility decline—which stretched from the late eighteenth century to the late 1940s baby boom that followed World War II—happened without any medical advance in contraceptive technology. In fact, it appears that the prevailing method was coitus interruptus, which is not only notoriously unreliable, but requires an unusual degree of personal discipline to be effective at all.

Current observations of nonindustrial societies generally support the link between industrialization and declining birth rates, since in the absence of rapid economic growth, family planning programs in countries such as India have been only marginally effective. The attempt by China to limit families to one child has apparently been flouted widely, especially in rural areas where children are most highly valued and state control is most difficult to assert. It is worth noting that governments have had even less success trying to promote fertility. At various points in their histories, for example, Germany, Japan, France, the Soviet Union, and Argentina have tried everything from cash rewards and subsidies to curbs on abortion to encourage large families, with very little success.

Industrial societies are now well into the third phase of the demographic transition, in which birth and death rates are low and roughly balanced, with natural increase rates close to zero and, in a few countries, negative. Although there was a baby boom following World War II in all industrial countries (as well as smaller "echo" booms since), demographers generally view these as temporary "blips" in an otherwise steady downward trend in fertility that has accompanied two centuries of industrialization. Most nonindustrial societies, however, are stuck in the second stage in which death rates are relatively low and birth rates—and, therefore, the rate of natural increase—are high. Why?

Death rates declined in Europe and the U.S. in the eighteenth and nineteenth centuries because of industrialization, which also affected birth rates. But third world countries have imported medical technology (such as vaccines against infectious disease) that lowers death rates without having the conditions of economic development and prosperity in which those discoveries were first made and which also supported declining fertility. As a result, although crude death rates are roughly the same in both industrialized and nonindustrialized countries, birth rates in nonindustrialized countries are more than twice as high and the rate of natural increase is four times as high.[18]

While many nonindustrial societies have managed to lower their birth rates somewhat over the last two decades, many have populations now so large that even moderately high rates of natural increase translate into enormous numbers of new people each year. India, for example, has a 2.1 percent rate of natural increase per year, about half that of the highest growth countries. Nonetheless, with a population of 850 million people, a 2.1 percent rate of natural increase results in almost 18 million additional people each year—a number that equals or exceeds the populations of ninety of the world's countries and just about equals the entire population of the state of New York. China, with a growth rate of just 1.4 percent, adds almost 16 million people each year. Clearly, even with declining birth rates, the numbers game of population growth is stacked against countries representing the

---

[18]The crude death rate is low in nonindustrial societies not only because of improvements in health care but also because their high fertility results in a large percentage of the populations falling in the childhood ages which typically have relatively low mortality. For this reason, crude death rates are not a valid indicator of the health of a population. Preferable measures are age-standardized death rates, the infant mortality rate, and life expectancy.

greatest concentrations of world population, and as we will see later, it is a game they cannot afford to lose.

Fertility as a
Social Process

One of the most fundamental sociological insights is that all behavior depends to some degree on the positions people occupy in social systems. Demographers have for many years used this insight in studying fertility differentials, especially by race, religion, and socioeconomic status. In the United States, for example, fertility rates for whites are consistently lower than for African-Americans, although racial differences shrink dramatically when we compare those with comparable education, occupation, marital status, and income. Indeed, once these variables are controlled, racial differences in the number of children couples say they *want* to have and the number they consider to be ideal virtually disappear, with some studies showing whites at the higher levels of education and occupation actually reporting slightly higher numbers than comparable African-Americans. Some of the racial differences in fertility that remains after controlling for other variables may have to do with the fact that whites tend to marry at older ages than African-Americans, which makes it easier to limit childbearing to the numbers couples intend to have.[19]

In addition to race, religious differences are often related to fertility. Jews, for example, have lower average fertility than either Protestants or Catholics, in part because they are more highly educated and are more likely to live in urban areas, both of which are associated with lower fertility; but those with no religious affiliation have the lowest fertility of all. Higher fertility among Catholics is caused in part by their wanting a higher number of children, but it also appears to be related to having more unplanned children. As Catholics have made more widespread use of contraception, the number of unwanted births has declined and fertility differences between Catholics and others have narrowed.

Certainly the most consistent and dramatic fertility differentials are those by socioeconomic status (SES) which, depending on

---

[19]See Kenneth Kammeyer and Helen Ginn, *An Introduction to Population* (Chicago: Dorsey Press, 1986).

how SES is measured, can take a variety of forms. The most common pattern is an inverse relationship in which fertility declines as SES increases, but there are some interesting exceptions. In agricultural societies such as Thailand, India, and Iran, where children have economic value, studies found higher fertility among more prosperous landowners—who can afford better nutrition and health care—than among poorer farmers. In Indonesia, higher class families have more children not only because of better living conditions, but because wives in more prosperous families are less likely to work outside the home and more likely to have stable marriages. In virtually all known societies, women engaging in economically productive work is associated with lower fertility, except when work and child care are compatible, as is the case with agriculture.

Even in industrial societies there have been periods when fertility and SES were not inversely related. During the 1940s, for example, the U.S. trend was in the shape of a backwards "J"—fertility declined with increasing SES, then turned upward again among the wealthiest families. In Norway and Sweden during the 1930s, the relationship took the shape of a "U"—the smallest families were found in the middle class. And in a few studies of narrowly defined subgroups of populations, a positive relationship has been found. In the famous 1941 Indianapolis study, for example, SES and fertility were positively related among white urban Protestants who planned both the number and timing of their children (but not among those who planned just the number).[20]

When education is used as the primary measure of SES, an inverse relationship with fertility is usually found, but again with interesting exceptions that shed light on fertility as a social process. If we just compare literates with illiterates, literacy is associated with higher, not lower, fertility, most likely because this minimal difference in education brings with it better health and nutrition but not different values about family size and other structural factors that promote lower fertility. It is not until higher levels of education that the relationship of fertility with increased education assumes its typical inverse pattern. Another interesting exception is found among U.S. Catholics, where college education is

---

[20] Pascal Whelpton and Clyde V. Kaiser, "Social and Psychological Factors Affecting Fertility," *Milbank Memorial Fund Quarterly* 2, 1950.

associated with higher fertility, but only if the college is itself Catholic and, therefore, further inculcates Catholic ideology and values about such issues as fertility, contraception, and abortion.

In general, fertility is lower in urban than rural areas, because urban populations are better educated and the occupational structure of urban economies increases the costs of having children. Here, again, interesting exceptions prove the rule. The urban-rural fertility difference for African-Americans, for example, is smaller than we would expect, a finding that may be due to the effects of discrimination and other factors in denying them the full economic and educational advantages of urban life enjoyed by other groups. To the extent that urban African-Americans are not substantially better off than their rural counterparts, their fertility will remain relatively high. This pattern is also found in many economically underdeveloped societies such as Mexico and India in which overurbanization has produced vast urban slums with fertility that is just as high—and in some cases higher—than in rural areas.

Whether we compare societies or categories of people within them, the fundamental biological process of reproduction is profoundly influenced by the characteristics of social environments and the positions people occupy within them. This is no less true of the equally biological phenomenon of death.

Death as a
Social Process

Although we tend to associate rapid population growth with fertility, growth during the last two centuries owes more to changes in mortality. As we saw earlier, the population explosion in the second stage of the demographic transition was caused not by an increase in birth rates—indeed, birth rates either declined or remained stable—but by dramatic death rate declines due almost entirely to environmental improvements such as cleaner water, more effective sewage disposal, better nutrition, and personal hygiene. Unlike fertility, mortality rates historically have been easier to control because many major causes of death operate somewhat independently of individual behavior. Separating sewage and potable water systems in a community, for example, or draining swamps where mosquitoes breed can decrease dramatically the incidence of infectious disease with no changes in individuals' behavior patterns or values.

This is less true of causes of death that are prevalent in industrialized countries, which by now have largely eradicated infectious diseases such as cholera and tuberculosis. In Japan, Europe, and North America, most people die from chronic conditions such as heart disease, stroke, and cancer, and violent causes such as homicide, suicide, and accidents—which are closely linked with individual behavior and circumstances such as diet, smoking, alcohol consumption, stress, occupational hazards, access to health care, and genetic predispositions. In the United States, for example, there has been a steady decline in deaths from heart disease and stroke, due at least in part to declines in cigarette and alcohol consumption and changes in diet. In the Soviet Union, however, deaths from heart disease, stroke, and respiratory cancer have actually increased over the past few decades to some degree because of very high rates of cigarette smoking and drinking.[21]

What is most interesting to sociologists is the connection between culture and social structure on the one hand and levels and causes of death on the other. Although everyone must die sometime, there is great variation in the ages at which people die and the conditions that cause it, which means that when and how we die depends to a considerable degree on the society we live in and our structural locations in it. Death is a socially structured phenomenon that illustrates the vital interface between our lives as biological and social beings. This is particularly true of the relationship between mortality and gender.

Almost without exception, females have lower death rates than males at every age of life and for all causes of death (the obvious exceptions being breast cancer and complications of pregnancy and childbirth). Although there are cases in which female death rates are higher than those for males, these are most likely due to social causes. In some nonindustrial societies, for example, infant mortality is greater among females, but only because the higher value placed on male children in patriarchal societies leads to female infanticide. Another case of Kennedy's

---

[21] For detailed information on death rates in the U.S., see the annual volumes published by the National Center for Health Statistics, *Vital Statistics of the United States* (Washington, DC: U.S. Government Printing Office). For information on mortality in the Soviet Union, see Richard Cooper, "Rising Death Rates in the Soviet Union," *The New England Journal of Medicine* 304,21 (May 1981): 1259–65; and John Dutton, "Changes in Soviet Mortality Patterns, 1959–1977," *Population and Development Review* 5,2 (June 1979): 267–91.

well-known study of mortality in Ireland from 1871 to 1962, in which he found that although females lived longer than males on the average, their advantage was much less than one would normally expect. He attributed this to the low standing of women in Irish society—their heavy burden of labor on farms and the preferences given to males in the distribution of food, shelter, health care, and clothing.[22]

Since males are more likely to die than females in utero, there may be biological differences that render males more vulnerable. For example, females have YY chromosome pairs and males have XY pairs. A genetic flaw in a female's Y chromosome is likely to have less of an effect since she has a second Y chromosome in the pair to back it up; but a flawed Y chromosome in a male can have more serious consequences since the remaining chromosome is an X and cannot therefore make up for the lost or damaged genetic information.

Aside from genetically-linked conditions, such as hemophilia and color blindness that are more common in males, not long after birth differences emerge that almost certainly reflect the influence of gender roles on health-related behavior. By adolescence, for example, male death rates from accidents—automobile accidents in particular—are many times higher than those for females, and by late adolescence and early adulthood, death rates from suicide and homicide are also substantially higher for males. By middle age, gender differences in death rates from cancer and heart disease widen steadily, partly due to a longer history of heavy cigarette smoking in the male population.[23] If recent trends are any indication, the increase in cigarette smoking among women over the last several decades will now take its toll as cancer death rates rise for women in dramatic contrast to an otherwise consistent pattern of declining or stable death rates for other causes.

A conclusive explanation of gender differences in mortality is still elusive, but there is good reason to argue for a substantial social component. Men, for example, are more likely to engage in physically hazardous occupations, take physical risks, and act out aggressive impulses (especially while driving cars). Men are less

---

[22] Robert E. Kennedy, Jr., *The Irish: Emigration, Marriage, and Fertility* (Berkeley: University of California Press, 1973).

[23] Samuel Preston, in fact, goes so far as to argue that cigarette smoking explains almost the entire gender differential in mortality. See "An International Comparison of Excessive Adult Mortality," *Population Studies* 24 (1970): 5–20.

likely than women to see physicians when they are not feeling well, which means that life-threatening conditions will be diagnosed at later and less treatable stages of development. Also, men are not only heavier smokers, but also heavier consumers of alcohol and addictive drugs.

There is debate about whether some roles performed primarily by men are accompanied by higher levels of stress. However, contrary to popular stereotypes, recent research shows that the highest stress levels are not found among male or female business executives but among their (largely female) secretarial and clerical workers, whose jobs combine high pressure to perform with little autonomy or control over their work. Nor are many men caught in the considerable role conflict and strain faced by both married and unmarried working mothers who are typically held responsible for child care, domestic work, and their jobs. This does not mean that pressures men experience are inconsequential, but it does suggest that stress accompanying men's roles is an unlikely explanation of gender mortality differentials. More likely is the possibility that men and women respond differently to stressful situations—that, for example, men's general unwillingness to express feelings of fear and vulnerability or to reach out for help, coupled with a general lack of intimate, supportive friendships makes them more vulnerable to the long-term debilitating effects of chronic unresolved stress.

As with fertility, one of the most striking mortality patterns centers on differences in socioeconomic status. Max Weber's use of the phrase "life chances" to describe a key dimension of social class has, in the eyes of demographers, a literal truth, for class characteristics such as education, occupation, and income consistently produce differences in health and longevity. Among people in families with incomes below $10,000 in 1989, for example, only 20 percent said they were in excellent health, compared with 52 percent of those earning $50,000 or more.[24] Similar differences exist between college graduates and those with less than high school educations, as well as between occupants of high and low prestige occupations. For mortality, those with the highest levels of education generally have death rates one-third lower than those

---

[24] Computed from General Social Survey data gathered by the National Opinion Research Center, University of Chicago.

with the least education, and those in the highest income groups have death rates two-thirds lower than those in the bottom income groups.[25]

The explanation of class differences in health and mortality involves both behavior and the resources that go with class position. In the working and lower classes, for example, men in particular are more likely to smoke cigarettes and consume more alcohol in comparison with those in higher classes. With fewer financial resources, they also have less access to health care and the necessities of life—food, shelter, clothing, and heat. They are far more likely to work in hazardous occupations, exposed to the dangers of injury and black lung disease associated with mining; injuries suffered in construction work, oil drilling, lumbering, and trucking, and working with machinery in factories; the risks of emphysema and other respiratory disorders caused by working in cotton mills; and exposure to cancer-causing chemicals, lead, and asbestos in both the chemical and construction industries. Add to these the occupational stress associated with jobs that offer little sense of autonomy or control over work, and the class structure is bound to produce differences in health even in the most medically advanced societies such as the United States and, with them, mortality differences as well.

Racial differences in health and mortality are striking and most certainly bound up in the dynamics of social inequality. In comparison with whites, African-American age-adjusted death rates range from 20 to 80 percent higher for heart disease, stroke, cancer, pneumonia and flu, accidents, and cirrhosis of the liver. For homicide, African-American rates are almost six times higher for males and four times higher for females. The infant mortality rate is 75 percent higher than among whites. The only major cause of death for which African-American rates are lower than for whites is suicide. Overall life expectancy was six full years lower than for whites in 1986, the second consecutive year in which life expectancy for African-Americans actually *declined* at the same time it increased for whites, a phenomenon that never happened before

---

[25] Sherwin Rosen and Paul Taubman, "Changes in the Impact of Education and Income on Mortality in the U.S.," In Linda DelBene and Foritz Schueren, eds., *Statistical Uses of Administrative Records with Emphasis on Mortality and Disability Research* (Washington, DC: Department of Health, Education and Welfare, Social Security Administration, Office of Research Statistics, 1979).

in this century.[26] Most of the decline is attributable to increased deaths from homicide, AIDS, and automobile accidents.[27]

While the most important mortality differentials have strong links with social inequality, some of the most interesting do not. For example, those who are married have lower death rates than those who are not, with the largest advantage being in a comparison with those who are widowed or, especially, divorced. Mortality differences are strongest for causes of death most directly related to personal behavior—suicide, homicide, accidents, and, to a lesser degree, lung cancer and cirrhosis of the liver. By comparison, leukemia death rates do not differ very much at all.[28]

An obvious explanation is that married life offers a more stable life, people are less likely to act in self-destructive ways, and are more likely to receive caring support for their emotional and physical well-being. This not only makes a great deal of sense—given the primacy of marital ties in the lives of most adults—but is also supported by research that shows the importance of all kinds of social ties in maintaining health. One study found, for example, that unmarried people who enjoy a close network of friends and relatives have death rates very similar to those of married people.[29]

Before we conclude that marital status per se causes differences in health and longevity, however, we have to consider the possibility that the differences we observe are due to other factors related to both marital status and mortality. In technical terms, we have to entertain the idea that the marital status effect on mortality is spurious—which is to say, it has to do more with statistical accident than cause and effect. We know, for example, that widowed and divorced people are older than those who are married, which raises the distinct possibility that married people have lower death rates not because they are married, but because

---

[26] Life expectancy is a statistical measure that indicates how many years a hypothetical group of people would live on the average if the age-specific death rates for a particular year—such as 1986—remained in effect over their entire lifetime.

[27] National Center for Health Statistics, reported in the *New York Times*, December 20, 1988, p. C14.

[28] See Walter R. Gove, "Sex, Marital Status, and Mortality," *American Journal of Sociology* 79,1 (July 1973): 45–67.

[29] Lisa F. Berkman and S. Leonard Syme, "Social Networks, Host Resistance, and Mortality: A Nine-Year Follow-up Study of Alameda County Residents," *American Journal of Sociology* 109,2 (1979):186–203.

they are younger (although this would not explain why death rates for married people tend to be lower than for those who have never married). We can test this by comparing death rates for people who differ on marital status but are the same age. When we do so, we find that the mortality differences are still there, which means that at least as far as age is concerned, the relationship between marital status and mortality is not spurious.[30]

There is, however, the less easily dismissed possibility that since entry into all statuses—including married, divorced, and so on—involves social selection, there are at least some differences between those whose marriages end and those whose endure, or between those who have married and those who have not. Furthermore, it is reasonable to argue that at least some of these differences are related to health—that people in poorer health or who lead less healthy lives are less likely to marry than those who do not, or, once married, are less likely to remain so.[31] At this point, it is impossible to tell how much of the marital status effect on mortality is due to differences in marital status per se or to differences in related variables such as social selection, but it is reasonable to assume for the time being that both factors are probably involved to some degree. In terms of sociological thinking, what is perhaps most important is the awareness that spuriousness is always a possibility and that differences between groups need have nothing to do with the characteristics of the groups themselves.

The explanation of differences between groups and social categories—such as those defined by age, race, gender, social class, and marital status—is, of course, at the heart of sociological analysis, and in addition to the ubiquitous possibility of spuriousness, mortality differentials illustrate two other important principles involved in that process. First, differences that apply generally to groups usually do not apply in all circumstances, and these exceptions can raise important questions of their own. In the case of mortality, differences between social categories usually do not hold for all causes of death. Although whites suffer from far higher

---

[30] Gove, op. cit.

[31] Given, however, trends of the past decade in which increasing numbers of young men and women are delaying marriage if not forgoing it altogether for a variety of reasons that have little to do with the "marriage market," it will be interesting to see if and how marital status differences in health and mortality change over the long run.

suicide rates than African-Americans, for example, they have considerably lower homicide death rates; and although married women generally have lower death rates than never-married women, the difference is reversed for homicide, automobile accidents, and—after the age of 45—cirrhosis of the liver.[32] Differences between categories can also vary considerably by factors such as age. As white women age, for example, their suicide rates peak around age 55 and then decline, but the rates for white men continue to rise steadily, producing differentials that widen dramatically with advancing age. Among African-American men and women, the suicide pattern by age is similar to that for white women, but with the peak occurring roughly twenty years earlier. As a result, among the very old suicide is a cause of death restricted almost entirely to white males.

A second principle is that differences between groups often do not hold equally for all of their subgroups. Several indicators, for example, suggest that while married people seem healthier than the unmarried, the benefits accrue far more to married men than to women and in many cases the marital advantage is reversed among women. Married women typically report higher levels on various measures of psychological distress such as nervousness and insomnia than single women, while the difference is just the opposite for men.[33] Widowed and divorced men are four times more likely to commit suicide than married men, but the gap for comparable women is considerably smaller. And as we saw earlier, for several causes of death married women are more vulnerable than never-married women. The identification of these kinds of variations and exceptions does not necessarily detract from the higher-level generalization. In most cases, it reveals the deeper complexity of social life, that we do not occupy one status at a time; we occupy combinations that can produce joint effects quite different from what we would expect from them singly or as a simple sum.

The Social Effects of Migration

Although birth and death rates certainly receive the most attention from demographers and the general public, migration

---

[32] Gove, op. cit.

[33] Reported in Jessie Bernard, *The Future of Marriage* (New York: Bantam, 1972).

has in many ways faster and more profound effects on social systems. It was primarily through migration, for example, that cities came into being and emerged as a dominant form of community life, and it is still migration that shifts the size and composition of populations over the short run and, in many cases, the long run as well. At the beginning of the twentieth century, immigration accounted for as much net population growth in the United States as natural increase did, if not slightly more.[34] The dramatic shifts in the distribution of the U.S. population—rapid growth in western and southwestern states, for example—is due not to different rates of natural increase, but to migration. And late in this century, the most difficult population questions in the U.S. focus not on natural increase or its components, but illegal immigration from third world countries—Mexico in particular.

In some cases, migration is prompted by natural disasters and other environmental changes that make relocation a matter of survival; but all other migration patterns are socially constrained to some degree.[35] At one extreme is forced migration, such as importing Africans as slaves into the Western Hemisphere, the relocation of American Indian tribes in the 1830s, the internment of Japanese Americans during World War II, or the deportation of tens of thousands of foreign workers from Nigeria in 1983. Less overtly coerced is migration in response to socially threatening conditions, such as the flight of Jews from Europe in the years prior to World War II, the migration of political refugees from Southeast Asia and Latin America, or the flight of tens of thousands of Turks from Bulgaria in early 1989 and thousands of East Germans into the West later that year. At the other end of the continuum is what Petersen calls free migration—when people personally choose to move, to marry, change jobs, attend graduate school, retire, and so on. While such moves are free in that they lack a threat or coercion, they are not free of social constraints. Like all social behavior, migration occurs as a choice among socially constructed and structured alternatives. The fact that Americans typically move following a marriage, for example, is not simply a matter of personal choice; it is a pattern of migration deeply tied to the

---

[34] For an excellent source for this and other historical statistics, see U.S. Department of Commerce, *Historical Statistics of the United States, Colonial Times to 1970* (Washington, DC: U.S. Government Printing Office, 1975), Parts 1 and 2.
[35] The types of migration described below are drawn from Petersen's typology of migration. See William Petersen, "A General Typology of Migration," *American Sociological Review* 23 (1958):256–65.

nuclear family model, the structure of work opportunities in industrial capitalist societies, and a culture that values independence and individualism. That people in agricultural societies are not as likely to move is no less connected to extended families, economic structures that attach fewer incentives and greater costs to migration, and cultures that place a relatively high value on community ties.

Understandably, most sociological attempts to explain migration focus not on coerced migration—whose causes are apparent—but on movement whose social causes are less visible. Most migration theories—from Ravenstein's classic nineteenth century analysis to late twentieth century efforts to explain migration of workers across national boundaries—approach migration as a response to changing economic and family conditions.[36] People move in response to changes in family composition over the life course or in response to declining work opportunities in one region and perceived opportunities in another. In the early 1900s, for example, the mechanization of agriculture and the resulting decline in the demand for labor was a major reason African-Americans began a long-term exodus from the South to a perceived racially tolerant and economically more promising North. Over the course of roughly half a century, the percentage of African-Americans living in the South dropped from 90 to 50 percent, but by the 1970s the flow reversed as thousands returned to the South in search of cheaper living conditions, better economic opportunities, and closer connections with kin in what they perceived to be a South where the racial atmosphere had improved considerably.[37]

Many migration theories focus primarily on factors that affect individual and family decision making—such as the desire for upward mobility—with less attention to the larger structural forces that create social situations in which migration becomes a viable if not attractive option. An interesting exception is some recent work trying to link international migration flows with

---

[36] See, for example, E. G. Ravenstein, "The Laws of Migration," *Journal of the Royal Statistical Society* 48, Part II (1885):61–235, and "The Laws of Migration," *Journal of the Royal Statistical Society* 52 (1889):241–305, both of which are surprisingly relevant a century later. See also Everett Lee, "A Theory of Migration," *Demography* 3 (1966):47–59; D. S. Massey, "Dimensions of the New Immigration to the United States and Prospects for Assimilation," *Annual Review of Sociology* 5(1981):57–85; and D. S. Massey et al., *Return to Aztlan: The Social Process of International Migration from Western Mexico* (Berkeley: University of California Press, 1987).

[37] U.S. Census Bureau, reported in the *New York Times*, June 11, 1989, p. 36.

changes in the world economy. Cheng and Bonacich, for example, argue that the dynamics of world capitalism promote migration of workers from poor, nonindustrial, peripheral areas such as Latin America and Southeast Asia to core industrial centers such as the U.S. and Europe.[38] This occurs for two reasons, both affected by the relationship between capitalists and workers.

As capitalism becomes more fully developed in core societies, workers become less productive away from the job (growing their own food or making their own clothes, for example) and more dependent on wages to meet their needs. In addition, the supply of cheap domestic labor declines as more and more people are drawn into the wage labor force. Together, these increase demands for higher wages, prompting capitalists to look outside their own societies for less expensive labor.

At the same time, the incursion of capitalism into nonindustrial societies disrupts local economies, creating widespread unemployment and otherwise making it difficult for people to meet their needs at home. In Latin America, for example, many economies have been transformed from largely subsistence farming in which people meet basic needs by growing corn and beans, for example, to cash market economies that export crops and require workers to meet their needs by working for wages. This results in large numbers of indigenous workers who migrate both to survive and to send money to the families they leave behind. This is precisely what many Mexicans have done in migrating to the United States.

Understanding worker migration by viewing the entire world as a single economic system is useful because it focuses on large-scale social forces that create conditions in which migration is both encouraged and perceived as a viable option, and it illuminates connections between individual choices and the larger social context in which they are made.[39] To focus entirely on the

---

[38] Lucie Cheng and Edna Bonacich, *Labor Immigration under Capitalism: Asian Workers in the United States before World War II* (Berkeley: University of California Press, 1984).

[39] This approach is known more formally in sociology as "world system theory" and derives primarily from the work of Immanuel Wallerstein. See, for example, his *The Modern World System* (New York: Academic Press, 1976); *The Capitalist World Economy* (Cambridge: Cambridge University Press, 1979); and *The Modern World System II: Mercantilism and the Consolidation of the European World Economy, 1600–1750* (New York: Academic Press, 1980). For an interesting criticism of this point of view, see Daniel Chirot, *Social Change in the Modern Era* (San Diego: Harcourt Brace Jovanovich, 1986).

personal reasons that underlie migration decisions ignores the crucial sociological fact that personal decisions are always constrained and conditioned by institutional arrangements and historical forces.

The Social Effects of Age Structure

For social systems, the dynamics of population growth and distribution take many forms. Changes in birth rates, for example, affect not only a population's rate of growth, but its age structure. Countries with high birth rates tend to have very young populations just as countries with low birth rates—virtually all of Europe and, increasingly, the United States—have relatively large percentages of elderly people. In most third world countries, for example, roughly half of the population is under the age of 15, compared with a quarter or less in industrial countries. At the other end the differences are reversed, with roughly 15 percent of populations over the age of 65 in industrial societies compared with 5 percent or less in the third world.

Age structure, in turn, affects social systems in many ways, from the level of crime (since young males produce far more than their proportionate share of crime) to the allocation of resources (between health care and schools, for example) and the availability of people to occupy social positions available to some age groups more than others. The dearth of teenage workers in the United States resulting from the end of the baby boom in the late 1960s has created a desperate situation for many competitive industries, such as fast food restaurants and mass market retailing (who are turning to the elderly to replenish their work force), and for the first time in the history of higher education, many colleges and universities are mounting serious advertising campaigns to attract applicants from a steadily shrinking pool of 18 to 24 year olds and are increasing their focus on adult students returning to school. In the 1990s, however, birth rates may increase for women in their early 30s who had postponed childbearing in order to pursue careers, and since these women are particularly likely to return to work shortly after giving birth, this threatens to overwhelm an already inadequate daycare system.[40]

---

[40] U.S. Census Bureau in the *New York Times*, June 22, 1989, p. A16.

The Problem
of Overpopulation

Certainly the best known and most serious effect of population growth and distribution on social systems lies in the balance
between the needs and resources of systems on the one hand and
the size and demographic characteristics of populations on the
other. The problems of overpopulation in the world as a whole,
and third world countries in particular, are by now well known
and are routinely linked to problems of economic development
and well-being. The fifteen poorest countries of the world contain
almost half of the world's population, and countries containing
the bottom 80 percent share a meager 25 percent of all world
income. In many third world countries, per capita income has
declined, with the prospect that income levels will fall below even
1960 levels.[41] Since the 1980s the problem of third world debt to
western banks has reached crisis proportions and not only
confronts banks with the specter of default, but creates widespread
unrest and violence in countries such as Argentina, whose
debt-repayment plans include substantial cutbacks in standards of
living.

Most approaches to the challenges of overpopulation follow
the "modernization" model, which views rapid population growth
as a primary impediment to economic growth. There are simply
too many people, and poverty will persist until birth rates fall
substantially below their present levels—even, perhaps below
replacement level (as China's one-child policy illustrates). This is a
somewhat refined application of Thomas Malthus's eighteenth
century observation that although food supplies tend to grow
arithmetically, population grows geometrically and, unless nature
or society intervenes to limit births or increase deaths, an
imbalance is inevitable.[42]

Although occasional technological advances may increase
food supplies dramatically, it is difficult to argue with Malthus's
basic ecological proposition that population size and the ability to

---

[41] The World Bank, *World Development Report 1983* (New York: Oxford University
Press, 1983). For figures on per capita income, see also annual editions of U.S.
Census Bureau, *Statistical Abstract of the United States* (Washington, DC: U.S.
Government Printing Office).

[42] Thomas Malthus, *Essay on the Principle of Population* (New York: Modern Library,
1960. Original edition, 1798).

support it in a given environment have practical limits. In addition to imbalances between sheer numbers and resources, populations with high birth rates typically have large percentages of children; and children are relatively unproductive and claim resources that otherwise could be invested in economic development and expanded production. These imbalances are exacerbated by migration patterns that swell already crowded cities such as Bombay and Mexico City with unskilled workers for whom no jobs, and a dwindling supply of basic services and resources such as sanitation and potable water, are available.

As much sense as the modernization approach makes, it has problems. Our understanding of the demographic transition argues that declining birth rates are as much a consequence as a cause of economic development, if not more so. Typical families in colonial America had six or seven children (far more than in most economically underdeveloped countries today) and declines took place largely in response to the shift towards industrialization and away from agriculture. Although national efforts to lower fertility in the absence of industrialization have had some limited effects, there is no reason to believe this will ever be enough to limit births all by itself.

The political implications of different approaches to population issues are still being debated. From an ecological perspective, overpopulation is not simply a matter of population alone, but concerns an imbalance between interrelated factors. One might argue—as some demographers have—that overpopulation is caused as much by an imbalance of wealth and resources in the world economic system as by sheer numbers of people in poor countries. China contains 21 percent of the world population, and yet consumes less than 10 percent of world energy expenditures. By comparison, the United States has 5 percent of world population, yet consumes 25 percent of its energy. Which society, then, places a greater population burden on the world—China with its billion people who consume very little or the United States with only a quarter as many people who nonetheless consume five times as much?

If we look at the world as a social system,[43] efforts to control population growth in the third world cannot be separated from the reality that social inequality between wealthy and poor countries

---

[43] See Wallerstein, op. cit.

constitutes a barrier to economic growth, a barrier that did not confront today's industrial societies when they first industrialized—at that time, lowering birth and death rates and, ultimately, rates of natural increase. Since these historical conditions are unlikely to occur again, it is difficult to see how third world countries will substantially improve their standards of living without changes in the world economic order *and* population control. It is sociologically and demographically naive to argue that one of these factors alone will be sufficient; but thus far, only the latter has received serious attention. It is unclear what it will take to raise and pursue serious questions about the former.

The Microecology of Social Interaction

Although sociologists usually focus on the dynamics of population and human ecology at the level of communities and societies, an entire area of study—what might be called microecology—focuses on how populations and the uses of physical space affect social interaction on smaller scales. The size of groups, for example, affects interaction patterns in many ways, from the level of social cohesion and the amount of satisfaction people feel to the ability of groups to make decisions and solve problems. Coalitions can exist only in groups of three or more people, which is why the potential for conflict is so much greater in groups of three than dyads, and why the addition of a child to a marriage can create problems between husbands and wives. Small groups tend to be more stable than large groups, more effective in solving problems that require creativity, and less likely to have leaders. Large groups, on the other hand, do better with tasks that require a variety of skills, solve problems with single solutions more effectively than smaller groups, and are more likely to have a leadership structure. Although we think of small groups as safer than large groups, at least some research suggests the intimacy of small groups inhibits the expression of potentially disruptive feelings such as anger and contempt.

The distribution of people in physical space has many effects on social relationships that we often overlook, from Virginia Woolf's classic argument that the dearth of women writers and artists is in part because women have had no rooms of their own in which to work, to the effects of architecture on interaction and friendship, and to the special dangers of warfare in which enemies can attack one another at great distances that insulate them from the suffering they cause. The physical distances that separate people in social relationships and the ways in which they are arranged vary predictably according to the type of relationship and the culture in which it exists.[44] That classrooms, courtrooms, and cathedrals share similar layouts—with rows of seating all facing front—is no accident and serves, among other purposes, to both focus attention and reinforce differences in authority. And that the family is perhaps the most frequent setting for violence in the U.S. is due at least in part to physical characteristics that include the sheer proximity and availability of family members for physical contact of all kinds, as well as the relative invisibility of behavior to outsiders who might intervene.

What is most sociologically interesting about these kinds of connections is the relationship between physical space on the one hand and the cultural and structural characteristics of social systems on the other. From the effects of racial and gender segregation to the design of office space to the separation of spouses in commuter marriages, physical arrangements can reinforce as well as undermine everything from the structural distribution of power to cultural stereotypes to the cohesion of social relationships.

Regardless of the scale of social life, attention to the dynamics of ecology and population is a much needed element of sociological thinking that is all too infrequent in sociological work. Without it, we too easily forget how physical human life is, from the processes of birth and death and the sensory basis of human experience to the ecological settings in which social systems develop and change, and social life unfolds. The incorporation of population and ecology into the core of sociological analysis provides an important grounding in the material realities of individual and collective human life.

---

[44] Probably the best discussion of this kind of analysis is still Robert Sommer, *Personal Space: The Behavioral Analysis of Design* (Englewood Cliffs, NJ: Prentice-Hall, 1969).

CHAPTER FIVE

— ◆ —

Thinking Sociologically

— ◆ —

Theoretical Frameworks

Sociological thinking requires a sensitivity to the existence of social systems and their cultural, structural, population, and ecological characteristics. These basic characteristics — and concepts such as value, role, and group that are related to and derived from them — make up a conceptual framework we can use to observe the world in a sociological way. This kind of framework is the foundation of any discipline, because it defines basic subject matter, whether it be the origins of the universe, the properties of living organisms, or the varieties of family life.

Although they sensitize us to perceive the world in particular ways,[1] these concepts are only the beginning of what is meant by sociological thinking, because a conceptual framework is only a point of departure to answer questions of what can be known about social life and alternative ways of coming to know it. We could, for example, use basic sociological concepts to describe the differences between industrial and nonindustrial societies, just as we could describe differences between various types of family systems, including the division of labor between men and women within families, how stable and enduring they are, and the incidence of various kinds of violence. But if we went no further than this, we would have said nothing about *why* such differences occur or what connections link them together. What, for example, are the social forces that bring industrialization about, and how do they and industrialization affect the family as an institution?

For these kinds of questions, mere description will not do. We can use concepts such as system and culture to become more aware about social systems and their various characteristics, but we also need frameworks that are theoretical—in other words, that organize how we think about social systems in order to explain what goes on in them. If conceptual frameworks direct our attention and tell us *what* to observe, theoretical frameworks tell us how to *interpret* and *understand* what we observe. The study of social systems requires a framework that includes basic assumptions about how they work and defines the kinds of questions we need to ask not only about how they work but also about the consequences they produce and how they change.

In the sociological literature you will not find a single unified theoretical perspective, for over the years sociologists have gone about this work in a variety of ways, resulting in several approaches, the most prominent being the functional, conflict, ecological, and interactionist perspectives. As is often the case in a discipline still establishing itself, the history of sociology includes a fair amount of disagreement among adherents to these several perspectives. Some of the issues have been primarily intellectual: Is social structure, for example, an external network of statuses and roles that shape human behavior, or is structure the actual patterns of behavior that result from what people do? Other issues have

---

[1] See Anthony Giddens, *The Constitution of Society: Outline of the Theory of Structuration* (Oxford: Polity Press, 1984), p. 326.

been as much political as intellectual: Is the conflict perspective superior because it reveals conditions of inequality and injustice, or does it lend itself to such excesses of advocacy of radical social change that it loses its intellectual usefulness? Does the functional framework support the status quo and, therefore, social inequality and injustice? Do we have to choose one or the other?

While these continuing arguments have their place, the purpose here is to spell out the basic kinds of intellectual work involved in sociological thinking, and in the process draw in the most useful parts of existing perspectives without engaging in or trying to resolve the ongoing debates among them. However much disagreement there may be among adherents to the various approaches, they are all nonetheless fundamentally sociological, and it is this common ground that I want to describe, if only in a rough way.

Social Systems and Their Consequences

As we saw in Chapter 1, at the heart of sociological thinking is the basic idea that social life is organized into systems whose characteristics shape the thoughts, feelings, experience, appearance, and behavior of the people who participate in them, just as those same people's behavior shapes those systems. Although it makes things analytically simpler to think of the characteristics of systems as separate and distinct from one another, they are themselves related in complex ways.

An industrial mode of production, for example, produces a great surplus of goods and services that not only supports a large population with a complex division of labor but also provides the material basis for structural inequality in the distribution of wealth, power, and prestige. Inequality is related to other structural factors (such as a division of labor that includes police and lawyers who can be used to protect the interests of privileged classes and suppress dissent), and to a variety of supportive cultural ideas such as the value placed on accumulating wealth or norms that protect private property. *A central problem in sociological thinking is to understand how these various characteristics of social systems operate to produce various kinds of consequences.*

Social systems produce several kinds of consequences. In the simplest sense, it is from people's participation in social systems that there emerges all of the patterns of how they think, know, feel, appear, experience, and behave. These are reflected in a wide range of indicators of collective experience and behavior, such as rates of morbidity, suicide, homicide, and other causes of death; rates of birth, marriage, divorce, abortion, sexual activity, book reading, tv and movie viewing, poverty, homelessness, employment, unemployment, economic production, commerce, financial activity, drug use, upward and downward mobility, political activity, warfare, migration, crime, and violence; average levels and inequality in the distribution of educational attainment, income, wealth, occupational prestige, health care, nutrition, and access to various social institutions such as the state, schools, and the legal system; consumption patterns of goods, energy, and other resources; and the generation and dissemination of ideas and other symbolic representations. All of this—from the recognizable patterned ways in which parents interact with their children to the relative levels of teenage pregnancy found in different societies—can be thought of as consequences of social systems.

Consider, for example, the fact that people in the U.S. are much less likely to vote than Canadians or Western Europeans.[2] This difference can be linked to several ways in which the U.S. political system discourages voting, especially among the working and lower classes that together include just under half of the adult population.[3] We can begin with the simple fact that voter registration is automatic in Canada but must be applied for in the U.S. and cannot be done at the polls. Since a fairly high percentage of U.S. *registered* voters in fact vote, it is reasonable to assume that to the extent that a system makes registration easy it facilitates and encourages voting.

On a deeper level, the U.S. political system is structured in ways that discourage voting by diluting the effect of voters' use of their franchise, especially for those whose views do not support the status quo. The system, for example, is organized around a winner-take-all principle that makes it virtually impossible for minority points of view to gain representation in either house of

---

[2] See F. F. Piven and R. A. Cloward, *Why Americans Don't Vote* (New York: Pantheon, 1988).

[3] See James A. Davis and Tom W. Smith, *General Social Surveys, 1972–1990: Cumulative Codebook* (Chicago: National Opinion Research Center, 1990).

Congress. In most European parliaments, seats are apportioned according to the percentage of the vote received by each party; but in the U.S., it is candidates, not parties, who are elected, and each seat is occupied by the candidate who wins a majority of votes. Under this system, it is theoretically possible for a party whose supporters accounted for just under half of the entire population to have no representation at all in Congress. In this way, anyone who favors a candidate who cannot win a majority of votes has little to gain from voting other than the moral satisfaction of having done one's duty, while the European voter knows that each vote will have a real additive effect on the representation of a particular point of view in government. As a result, many U.S. voters do not bother.

One could also argue that the U.S. political system discourages voting because it is organized around a two-party system that offers voters little choice on many fundamental issues. Although the Republican and Democratic parties differ on many specific issues such as abortion rights, they are quite similar in their support of the interests of capitalism, wealth, property, and the use of the military to further national interests. Since the costs of such policies are borne primarily by the working and lower classes, and since these people probably perceive that they will bear those costs regardless of which of the two major parties is elected, it is not surprising that they are especially unlikely to vote.[4] In the 1988 presidential election, for example, those who placed themselves in the middle class were 30 percent more likely to vote than those who placed themselves in the working and lower classes, and those whose incomes were $60,000 or more were 54 percent more likely to vote than those with incomes of $10,000 or less.[5]

To attribute the low and declining turnout of voters in U.S. elections to shared psychological conditions such as apathy is to miss the crucial sociological point that patterns of thought, feeling, and behavior are to a considerable degree produced by the characteristics of social systems. Indeed, one might argue that the system is constructed in a way that actively discourages voting and

---

[4]See R. Vanneman and L. W. Cannon, *The American Perception of Class* (Philadelphia: Temple University Press, 1987).

[5]Computed from General Social Survey data produced by the National Opinion Research Center, University of Chicago, James A. Davis and Tom W. Smith, principal investigators; analysis performed on MicroCase software, Cognitive Development, Inc., Seattle, WA.

that nonvoting is a rational response to that system—in which case the problem is not one of a lack of caring, socially induced or otherwise.

Some of the consequences produced by social systems take the form of various conditions in the systems themselves, such as the degree of strain, contradiction, cohesion, stability, integration, and conflict. The recent dramatic changes in Central Europe, for example, that led to the radical restructuring of one socialist government after another can be interpreted at least in part as a result of prolonged periods of authoritarian rule and failed economic policies that produced increasingly intolerable levels of strain and contradiction between the values espoused by political leaders and the realities of everyday life. One could look at the Great Depression of the 1930s in a similar way—the excesses promoted by industrial capitalism led to a collapse of the system and considerable structural and cultural change (such as the creation of Federal regulatory agencies and laws empowering them to control the stock market and the banking industry).

Social systems also produce consequences that affect other social systems. The Industrial Revolution, for example, radically altered the relationship of the family to production by moving production from the home to the factory. Among the many consequences of this was a new division of labor in families, with husbands becoming breadwinners and wives responsible for domestic work whose economically productive value was steadily eroded by the spread of factory-based production. As a social system, however, the family in turn affects economic systems. Declining wages in the 1980s, for example, coupled with changes in women's aspirations prompted by the women's movement, has caused a rapid growth in the percentage of families with both parents employed outside the home. This creates considerable strain within the family—especially around the issue of child-care—which, in turn creates pressures for the development of childcare services in the workplace as well as innovative ways of scheduling work.

As these examples suggest, every social system is nested in a larger network of systems, and what goes on in one cannot be fully understood without examining its relation to larger networks. Just as families in industrial societies are connected to larger systems (schools, economy, and the state, for example), these larger systems are also embedded in relationships with still larger systems—such as schools in relation to communities and the state or national economies in relation to the world economic system. The complexities of these relationships underscores the sociological importance of being able to shift back and forth between different levels of analysis, and being able to focus on a specific system, all the while maintaining an awareness of the larger social context in which and through which it exists. In this sense, a full sociological understanding of problems of psychological development encountered by today's children requires consideration not only of immediate factors such as their relationships with parents and siblings or their exposure to mass media and other cultural influences, but also relationships between families and economic institutions, schools, and day-care centers, and the relationships that connect these to local, state, and federal governments. Even these ultimately must also be related to still larger systems such as the world economic system, whose consequences profoundly affect the economics of everyday life. Whether children get what they need as they grow up depends not only on the resources and behaviors of family members, but in a larger sense on the limitations imposed on families by conditions in social systems extending far beyond their boundaries.

In addition to the complex relationships among social systems, it is also important to be aware that their consequences affect people differently depending on the positions they occupy in those systems. The United States, for example, has by far the highest homicide rate of any industrial society, with Finland providing the nearest competition with a rate only a third as large.[6] Within the U.S., however, there are striking patterns in the distribution of homicide according to social statuses such as race, gender, and age. Black males, for example, are nearly six times more likely to be murdered than white males or nonwhite females and 17 times more likely than white females.[7] Overall, males are more than three times as likely as females to be murdered, and infants under the age of one year are more than twice as likely to be murdered as are children 1 to 4 years old and more than five times as likely as are children 5 to 14 years old.[8]

---

[6]Rosemary Gartner, "The Victims of Homicide: A Temporal and Cross-National Comparison," *American Sociological Review*, 55,1 (1990).

[7]U.S. Department of Justice, *Criminal Victimization in the United States: 1988*, (Washington, DC: U.S. Government Printing Office, 1989).

[8]Gartner, op. cit., Table 1.

To account for such differences we must look again to the characteristics of social systems. Gartner, for example, studied homicide trends in developed nations, and found that rates increase with rising divorce rates, declines in welfare spending, and increases in social inequality. They also tend to be higher in countries with ethnically heterogeneous populations and high levels of official violence such as the imposition of the death penalty. She argued from these and other data that adult homicide rates are affected by economic inequality and the level of absolute deprivation in social systems as well as breakdowns in cohesion and the stability of major institutions such as the family.[9]

Similar kinds of analyses can be done for all the various consequences produced by social systems, from how schools affect the academic achievement of students of different races or social classes to the effects of capital punishment on rates of violent crime, to the consequences for family stability that result when both parents work outside the home. In each case the central sociological questions are the same: *what consequences are produced by social systems, how they are produced, and how are they experienced by the various categories of people who participate?*

Stability and Change

Although the use of the word "system" may suggest rigid stability, in reality social systems always exist in varying degrees of imbalance between forces of stability and change. If we look at social systems in terms of the people who participate in them, stability is maintained primarily by the socialization process, through which people are trained to accept the status quo and become dependent on it for their sense of identity and security. It is also maintained, however, by the ability of those in positions of power to coerce others, whether it takes the form of parental authority over children or the authority of the state to use armed force against its own citizens or external enemies. On the larger level of social systems taken as a whole, stability also depends on the interdependent connections among systems that make it difficult to change one without changing others. One of the difficulties involved with ending hostilities between the U.S. and

---

[9]Gartner, op. cit., p. 95.

the Soviet Union, for example, lies in the fact that the politics of military power are so closely tied to the economics of defense industry production which is, in turn, closely connected to the economic well-being of many states and communities, and the families that live and work in them.

Pushing against the forces of stability are conditions both within and external to social systems that impel them towards change. Perhaps the most sociologically interesting of these are the consequences produced by social systems themselves, such as strain, contradiction, anomie, lack of cohesion, instability, lack of integration, and social conflict, especially when accompanied by social movements such as those focusing on civil rights, women's rights, the environment, disarmament, poverty, nuclear power, abortion, and democracy. But to these we would have to add a host of other factors that promote change. Change, for example, often occurs in a social system in response to changes in other social systems, as in the case for West Germany in response to the breakdown of authoritarian government in East Germany, the tearing down of the Berlin Wall, and other social barriers between the two countries. Changes in the physical environment—such as natural disasters, pollution, and the destruction of forests—can result in dramatic changes in everything from the degree to which government regulates industry to the survival of entire communities. Population changes—such as changing rates of birth, death, growth, and migration, as well as changes in population size and age structure—can prompt a variety of social changes, from women entering the labor force in increasing numbers to the inability of communities to provide services for newly arrived migrants. For all of these, the fundamental sociological question remains the same: *How do social, population, and ecological conditions contribute to stability and change in social systems?*

People and Social Systems

A long-standing issue in sociological thinking is the relationship between people and social systems. Social systems would not exist without the participation of people, and yet people's perceptions, thoughts, feelings, appearance, behavior, and experience are undeniably shaped and constrained by social facts. This is clear in our dependence on language to represent and interpret reality and expectations. As we saw in Chapter 2, we use language as a way of imagining the inner life of others—their thoughts, feelings, and expectations—and, through this, we interpret and perform roles and develop a sense of self in relation to others. On this is based perceptions not only of other people but of social systems as a whole and social identity as defined by our positions in them.

The central connection between people and social systems exists through the roles associated with the statuses they occupy. Statuses and roles are the points at which people's otherwise private and isolated lives interact and overlap with social systems, with each affecting the other. What each of us perceives to be the social reality of a family, for example, shapes our perceptions, interpretations, expectations, and, ultimately, behavior. We all have ideas of what we think family life should be, from whether parents should use physical punishment to control their children's behavior to whether families should sit down and eat meals together. But as we then participate in that system, what was otherwise an abstract image in our minds and the minds of many others—"a family"—is rendered into a concrete reality of actual people living and behaving in relation to one another in a particular situation. The fit between the two—the social system as we perceive it and how people manifest it though their behavior— is, of course, far from perfect in the sense that we may have a great deal of latitude in deciding just how to perform a particular role. People may subscribe to the idea that families should eat meals together in order to promote a sense of intimacy, but the reality may be quite different, with each family member eating on a different schedule. There is, then, a dynamic relationship between social systems on the one hand and people on the other through which we can exercise varying degrees of power and influence over the nature of the social systems we participate in. We are both shaped by social systems and, through our behavior, shapers of them.

It is through our participation in social systems that we relate to other people, for it is through role relationships that our lives overlap and interact with the lives of others. This occurs on several different levels. In some ways, social interaction takes the form of exchanges through which we seek what we need and want in exchange for what we have to give. When we do favors for other people, for example, we may do so expecting that they will think better of us and will be more likely to act in a friendly way towards us in the future. From another perspective we can see how we use language, gestures, appearance, and behavior to create and sustain impressions of ourselves in the eyes of other people and to protect the integrity of our role performances. Bankers and professional comedians, for example, will dress, speak, and behave very differently because the roles associated with their statuses are very different; and when bankers behave in inappropriate ways they may use a variety of techniques to recover themselves and repair any damage done to people's impressions of them. A banker who makes jokes about the possibility of a bank failing in the near future, for example, or who pretends to pocket the cash you just deposited, may be quick to apologize or disown such behavior ("I was only kidding") or show signs of embarrassment that indicate the behavior was inappropriate and unlikely to be repeated.

In the most fundamental sense, social interaction cannot take place unless the participants share the belief that social relationships in fact exist and the expectations that go along with them are real and shared. People use a variety of generally unarticulated methods to create and sustain these shared impressions—various civil and religious rituals, for example, such as weddings, funerals, and holiday observances reinforce the shared perception that societies and communities continue to exist and cohere through sets of shared values and beliefs. On a less formal level, social interaction is full of ritualistic behavior, such as the exchange of greetings and inquiries about well-being that go with meeting others on the street, that have as their primary function the maintenance of a shared sense of social reality.

In order for people to participate in any of this, they of course have to undergo a considerable amount of socialization, acquiring a sense of themselves as social beings, and a perception of how social systems work and what is expected of those who participate in them in different positions. This is accomplished in many ways, including explicit instruction (such as in school), the use of punishment and reward, imitation of models, and exposure to representations of cultural ideas in such diverse forms as art, literature, the mass media, advertising, dance, music, and story-telling. A major result of all of this is that people acquire personal identities rooted in their membership in social systems, beginning with the family and extending to groups, organizations, communities, and societies. We define and see ourselves in such terms as daughter, student, Canadian, New Yorker, basketball player, Protestant, or clerk. The degree to which this occurs affects not only how much conformity there is in social systems, but also the extent of creativity, innovation, and nonconformity which may play important parts in bringing about social change.

The relationship between people and social systems and the patterns of interaction that result are very complicated, and draw sociological thinking towards questions about the nature of those relationships, how people are prepared to participate in them, and the dynamic mechanisms through which social interaction actually occurs.

The remainder of this chapter describes the major theoretical perspectives that have emerged over the last century and a half. Although they differ in many ways—and are used by many sociologists to organize their work—they have important elements in common that make them fundamentally sociological; and it is these elements that have been identified and brought together in the framework just outlined.

The Functional Perspective

The functional perspective—especially as developed by Émile Durkheim—was in part a reaction to the utilitarian thinking that dominated Europe at the time. Utilitarians explained social life as the sum of the rational calculations of individuals, with little sense that social systems and their problems might involve factors that existed apart from people's choices.

Partly in reaction to this view, Durkheim worked from the ideas that the whole is greater than the sum of its parts, and that the ways in which the parts of social systems are constituted and arranged affect both the nature of these systems and the behavior and experience of the people who participate in them. He borrowed heavily from the emerging field of biology and likened social systems to living organisms complete with organs (institutions) and normal and pathological states. Although the organismic model of society has long since been abandoned, it was an important transitional concept that helped establish the idea that social systems are entities that must be studied as such if we are to fully understand not only social life as a whole, but individual lives as well.

As one might expect, the primary focus of functional analysis is the social system as a system—how it works, how its various subsystems and characteristics contribute to the operation of the whole, how it is maintained and adapted to changing conditions, and the consequences it produces. Systems are seen as having various requirements in order to operate in particular ways, such as adaptability, stability, cohesion, coordination of their various parts, establishing and attaining goals, ensuring that people who participate in the system know their roles and are motivated to perform them, and managing or resolving conflict and strain that arise within the system or in relation to other systems.[10] In addition, all social systems include a set of cultural values that guide what goes on within them and in relation to other systems.

From this perspective, various aspects of social systems— from the rate of serious crime to the structure of a political party system—can be examined in terms of the consequences they produce and how these support or interfere with system requirements or values. Consequences that contribute to these are functional, while those that interfere are dysfunctional. Manifest consequences are intended and clearly identifiable parts of a system, while latent consequences are hidden and less easily anticipated or identified.[11]

The functional perspective sensitizes us to some of the most important aspects of social systems. By taking the system as the basic unit of analysis, it draws attention to the fundamental ways in which various social phenomena are interconnected, often in unanticipated ways. Historical changes in the family, for example—including lowered fertility, increased participation of women in the paid work force, and the increasing reluctance of both women and men to marry and form families—cannot be understood without seeing their connection with changes in economic systems, especially those brought about by industrialization as it has developed in both its capitalist and socialist forms. In similar ways, the work of scientists cannot be understood without paying attention to the connections between the social systems that produce scientific knowledge—such as universities and corporate research labs—and the economic, political, and military institutions that provide most funding for research.

---

[10] See Talcott Parsons, *The Social System* (New York: The Free Press, 1951).

[11] See Robert K. Merton, *Social Theory and Social Structure,* enlarged ed. (New York: The Free Press, 1968).

By approaching social life from a perspective that looks for interconnections within and between social systems, we become more aware of the consequences that these systems produce. Most important, we are compelled to look for the causes of social phenomena in the characteristics of social systems or, to paraphrase Durkheim, to search for the causes of social facts in relation to other social facts.[12] We might be able to explain why a woman is homeless purely on the basis of her individual choices and circumstances, for example, but as we saw in Chapter 1, we could never use this approach successfully to explain the *rate* of homelessness in the United States or why it is so much higher than in other industrialized societies. The central insight of the functional perspective is that characteristics of social systems—such as the rate of homelessness—can only be understood as the product of, and therefore in terms of, the cultural, structural, population, and ecological characteristics of those social systems and their relation to other social systems.

The functional perspective is an important resource for approaches to social problems, because it enables us to see why such problems are so difficult to solve. If poverty and homelessness were simply matters of skill, motivation, and so on, then their solution would be relatively simple. But if they are instead consequences of social systems that include entire societies and their major institutions as well as their relations to other societies, then their solution is a more difficult proposition involving far more than changing people's characteristics. Compared with overhauling entire political and economic systems—as many Central European societies are now discovering—the reeducation of a population is a relatively simple and straightforward task.

Functionalism's most important insight is that social systems exist as entities that must be understood in terms of their characteristics and the consequences they produce, including poverty, injustice, oppression, chaos, and conflict. By paying attention to the consequences produced by social systems we can see more clearly how even the most horrific social conditions are often grounded in the normal operation of a social system and as

---

[12] Émile Durkheim, *The Rules of the Sociological Method* (New York: The Free Press, 1938. Originally published by 1895).

such are connected with institutional arrangements that are generally not otherwise thought to be problematic.

The Conflict Perspective

The conflict perspective focuses on the important insight that control over social systems is often distributed unequally, that social systems can benefit the interests of some groups at the expense of others, and therefore often produce conflict and struggle over the distribution of resources and rewards and the terms on which people live. As it has developed since its nineteenth-century origins in the work of Karl Marx and, to a lesser degree, Max Weber and Georg Simmel, the conflict perspective emphasizes understanding how division and inequality are produced and how these affect social life.

To conflict theorists, societies are more often than not marked by systematic patterns of inequality and dominance by elite groups who manipulate and control major social institutions in their own interests.[13] Since institutions are often closely identified with the society itself, conflict theorists argue that what is considered normative for a society is often that which supports elite privilege and dominance, and the otherwise desirable goals of stability and social cohesion include the perpetuation of what is often an unjust and oppressive status quo. Indeed, elite interests can have negative if not disastrous consequences not only for subordinate groups but for entire societies. In the United States, for example, the most often identified indicators of a healthy economy are capital growth and profits, which do not include measures of the quality of life such as the availability of health care and affordable housing, adequate nutrition, an unpolluted environment, or safe workplaces. As evidence mounts of a decaying infrastructure, of

---

[13] This generalization applies only to societies of the last several thousand years. Feminist scholarship is gathering an impressive body of evidence that the vast majority of human experience—which is both prehistorical and prepatriarchal—was marked by egalitarianism, cooperation, and sharing. See, for example, Riane Eisler, *The Chalice and the Blade* (New York: Harper and Row, 1987). For a different type of analysis that shows the relationship between economic development and the existence of social inequality, see Gerhard Lenski, *Power and Privilege* (New York: McGraw-Hill, 1966).

declining effectiveness of schools, of increasing pollution, a serious drug problem, destabilized families, and the failure to substantially change the impoverished status of most categories of nonwhites, it becomes clear that the interests of elites can advance at the expense of society as a whole.

Although one does not have to be a Marxist to use the conflict perspective, his views are instructive. To Marx, industrial societies generate strain and conflict through economic arrangements in which the means of production are not held in common but are owned or controlled by a few who are in a position to exploit the many who work for them in return for wages. As recent events in Central Europe and the Soviet Union suggest, this is a problem in both socialist and capitalist societies, although in the former it is the state that controls the means of production, and generally not to enrich an elite. From a conflict perspective, these societies produce division and struggle, and the institutional forms of social life—from family dynamics to pop culture to international politics—are shaped by that struggle and the dominance by elites. Marx's view that everything of social importance flows from or is strongly influenced by economic forces rests on the assumption that there are distinct linear causes for social development and change; his theory builds upon this an optimistic view that revolutionary change is built into the economic structure of societies themselves.

Although Marx is the one most often associated with the conflict perspective, his materialistic view of societies is not the only approach. Max Weber, for example, argued that the mode of production was not the only—or even the most important—force in shaping social systems; and yet he, too, was deeply disturbed by nineteenth-century developments that threatened to increase the control of the few over the many, especially by the proliferation of bureaucratic organization. Weber was the first to describe in detail what he called the rationalization of social life through which efficiency, the calculation of costs and benefits, and the pragmatic consideration of means and ends were becoming dominant values threatening individual liberty and identity. Unlike Marx, Weber's view was a pessimistic one in which the bureaucratic model would be adopted by almost all institutions—business, government, religion, education, science, the military—a prediction that has, of course, proved to be quite accurate.

More recently, Ralf Dahrendorf has combined the perspectives of Marx and Weber by arguing that it is not the simple ownership or control of the means of production that causes conflict, but inequalities of power in the bureaucratic institutions through which so many aspects of social life—including production—are organized.[14] Since authority is in limited supply, argues Dahrendorf, it is inevitable that strain and conflict will arise between those who have more and those who have less, even though authority is a form of social power that by definition has social legitimacy. In this sense, Dahrendorf suggests that authority relations are a source of both social cohesion and integration on the one hand and conflict and division on the other.

It is important to be aware that like the functional perspective, the conflict perspective can be used at all levels of social life, from macro relations among societies to the micro level of role relationships. The nuclear family structure, for example, can be analyzed in terms of its effects on family interaction and the tendency of families to produce inequality, strain, and conflict. The ways in which strain, conflict, and the other aspects of human relationships are acted out in each family, however, is generally beyond the pale of the conflict perspective. For this we have to use a point of view with a finer screen through which to sift the characteristics and consequences of social systems—the interactionist perspective—to which we will turn shortly.

The Ecological Perspective

Although the functional and conflict perspectives dominate sociological thinking on the macro level, they are not alone in this area. In recent years there has been a resurging interest in the population-ecology perspective, a theoretical framework that has enjoyed a vigorous if somewhat indeterminate place in sociology for much of this century.

The population-ecology perspective rests on the central insight that all social systems involve some number of people who exist in relation to one another and physical surroundings. It is impossible to fully understand social systems without taking into account the characteristics of their populations—their size, com-

---

[14] See Ralf Dahrendorf, *Class and Class Conflict in Industrial Society* (Stanford, CA: Stanford University Press, 1959); "Toward a Theory of Social Conflict," *Journal of Conflict Resolution* 2 (June 1958):170–83.

position, and physical distribution—and the dynamic processes through which they change—fertility, mortality, and migration. Equally important are the complex ways in which social systems organize themselves to use technology and their physical environments to produce goods and services. The theoretical attempt to integrate population and environmental factors with structural and cultural aspects of social systems results in a four-part perspective that Duncan and Schnore summarize with the acronym POET—Population, Organization, Environment, and Technology.[15]

As we saw in Chapter 4, a major focus of the ecological perspective has been the social evolution of societies—the effects of technology and changing modes of production on societies and their institutions, from religion and the state to marriage and the family.[16] The primary concern is with the production of goods and services of all kinds (whether or not they have value in a cash market economy) and the flows of activity among various social systems through which production occurs. Each system draws inputs from the environment and other social systems, and then participates in the production, distribution, and consumption of outputs.[17]

This applies most obviously to economic production but also to the activities of other kinds of social systems as well. Families in industrial societies, for example, draw inputs from their surroundings, including the goods and services they buy. They use these to produce outputs, the most important of which are children, but also include services provided to family members, from the preparation of food to taking care of the sick or infirm. By comparison, families in nonindustrial societies differ sharply— they tend to be much larger, produce most of the goods they consume, occupy a far more central place in the life of their societies, and face few if any of the childcare dilemmas faced by working parents in the U.S. To a population ecologist, such differences cannot be understood simply in terms of culture and social structure since these are themselves connected with differ-

---

[15] Otis Dudley Duncan and Leo F. Schnore, "Cultural, Behavioral, and Ecological Perspectives in the Study of Social Organization," *American Journal of Sociology* 65 (1959).

[16] See, for example, Gerhard Lenski and Jean Lenski, *Human Societies: An Introduction to Macrosociology*, 5th ed. (New York: McGraw-Hill, 1987).

[17] Krishnan Namboodiri, "Ecological Demography: Its Place in Sociology," *American Sociological Review*, 53,4 (1990):619–33.

ences in the mode of production—industrial versus horticultural, for example—and the technology on which these differences rest.

The population-ecology perspective is especially useful for studying these kinds of problems, as well as for identifying and explaining shifts in the characteristics of populations and social systems. The causes and consequences of an aging population, for example, make up a classic sociological problem that is readily identified from this point of view. The history of the family is another area that falls easily within this frame of reference, since it involves changes in the number of children, the average size of households and families, and the relative numbers of different family and household types. In the U.S., the age at first marriage has been increasing steadily for some time as more and more young people delay marriage and live together without marrying. In addition, adults of all ages are increasingly likely to live alone, family size is shrinking, and the single-parent family is the fastest growing—and one of the most impoverished—of all family structures.

With its emphasis on the flows of activities that organize social systems and connect them to one another, and with its unique appreciation for the importance of numbers, growth, distribution, geography, technology, production, and the environment, the population-ecology perspective certainly deserves a place near the center of any sociological framework.[18] Like all macrolevel perspectives, however, it is less useful when it comes to understanding the microlevel details of social interaction. For this we must look to an entirely different set of theoretical perspectives that fall under the general heading of interactionist.

The Interactionist Perspective

While the functional, conflict, and ecological perspectives focus primarily on social systems and the consequences they produce, the interactionist perspective is concerned with how people actually behave in relation to one another within the general constraints that are themselves a consequence of social

---

[18] Ibid. See also Amos H. Hawley, *Human Ecology: A Theoretical Essay* (Chicago: University of Chicago Press, 1986).

systems. As such, the main theoretical problem among interaction-ists concerns the relationship between people and social systems.

Theorists who identify most closely with structural role theory emphasize that people's social positions limit their choices of how to appear and behave (not to mention how to perceive, think, and feel). The patterns of behavior that comprise social life are, from this perspective, quite stable and predictable because the expecta-tions they are based on are shaped by external social facts which are internalized to each individual's sense of a core self. This implies that the basic organization of social life consists of an arrangement of statuses and roles.[19]

One problem with this view is that much behavior is not linked to clearly defined statuses and roles. There are many situations in which expectations are loosely defined or unclear, and in which people primarily improvise and make up major portions of social reality as they go along. Herbert Blumer takes this observation a step further by arguing that not only is there a great deal of room in social life for this kind of improvisation, but what people actually do in their interactions with one another in fact lies at the center of what social systems *are*.[20] In his view, social structure is not external to individuals; indeed, it emerges from social interaction and does not otherwise exist.

In this sense, structure is less a set of purely external constraints than a continuing process through which social reality is created and recreated by people's appearance and behavior.[21] When customers and clerks interact in a store there are recogniz-able patterns of expectation that distinguish this situation from others—clerks are supposed to answer questions, for example, guard merchandise from theft, receive money in exchange for goods, and generally defer to customers' wishes whenever possi-

---

[19] For a summary of this disagreement among interactionists, see Bernard N. Meltzer and Jerome W. Petras, "The Chicago and Iowa Schools of Symbolic Interactionism," in T. Shibutani, ed., *Human Nature and Collective Behavior* (Engle-wood Cliffs, NJ: Prentice-Hall, 1970). See also Stanford M. Lyman and Arthur J. Vidich, *Social Order and Public Philosophy: An Analysis and Interpretation of the Work of Herbert Blumer* (Fayetteville and London: University of Arkansas Press, 1988); and Jonathan Turner, op. cit., Chapters 15 and 16.

[20] See Herbert Blumer, *Symbolic Interactionism: Perspective and Method* (Englewood Cliffs, NJ: Prentice-Hall, 1969). See also Meltzer and Petras, op. cit., and Lyman and Vidich, op cit.

[21] Thus—recalling the discussion of culture in Chapter 2—both culture and structure play important parts in the social construction of reality.

ble ("the customer is always right"). For their part, customers are expected to pay for any merchandise they take, refrain from damaging merchandise, try on clothing in designated private areas, and so on.

Expectations, however, are only abstractions until people begin to behave in relation to them and each other, sending symbolic cues and messages that indicate their understanding of the social facts that pertain to their situation. Although they act with some awareness of what is expected of them as clerks and customers, each decides how to interpret those expectations and, given them, what to do. "May I help you?" for example, is more than a simple question; it is a common phrase used to initiate a customer-clerk interaction. How that relationship emerges depends on how the customer chooses to respond. In doing so, every time a customer and clerk interact, the choices they actually make about what to do and say are what literally create the customer-clerk relationship anew, and without this continual re-creation, it would not exist. In this sense, structure is a process shaped through its dynamic relationship with interaction; but the interaction is also informed and shaped to some degree by shared perceptions of what that process is supposed to be. It is in this way that social life blends both improvisational unpredictability and recognizable patterned regularities.

The opportunities to improvise and create social reality are increased by the fact that role relationships rarely specify exactly what people are to say and do at every moment, which leaves varying amounts of room for individuals to interpret situations for themselves and, through their behavior, to literally create social reality. Whether doctors and patients discuss the weather, politics, or their personal lives, for example, is not specified by their roles, nor are the countless facial expressions and other gestures through which people convey feelings and thereby create impressions and expectations.

The argument over the relationship between social systems and interaction focuses on the basic relationship between what people do on the one hand and the patterned regularities that we think of as social systems on the other. How clearly structured and predictable is social life and how much of it is made up as we go along? Although each polar position has its proponents, it makes more sense to incorporate both into a single view of the relationship between people and social systems: We are not free of social constraints, and yet in our individual choices of how to perceive, interpret, and respond to those constraints, we recreate and shape them in ways that are only partially predictable.

As a perspective, interactionism developed along several lines. It began with philosopher George Herbert Mead, whose concepts of mind, self, and generalized other are part of the groundwork for a general view known as symbolic interactionism. This perspective recognizes the vital role played by symbols in the creation and acting out of social reality.[22] Its main focus is the ways in which talk and gestures are used to manifest, shape, and sustain what would otherwise be no more than a set of abstractions—culture and social structure.

As we saw in the discussion of Mead in Chapter 2, language plays a part in the creation of the self as well as in the presentation of ourselves to others. Language is the vehicle through which we discover the inner lives of others and, as a result, become aware of ourselves as selves. Erving Goffman's more recent dramaturgical perspective uses a framework in which everyday social interaction is likened to the theater, complete with actors, audience, scripts, and props.[23] In Goffman's view, role behavior is like a theatrical performance in front of others who function much like an audience, before whom we create and manage impressions of ourselves through our behavior, what we say, and how we appear. For its part, members of the audience not only witness a performance, but engage in performances of their own, which means that everyone is always both performer and audience.

When a man and a woman go out on a date, for example, each pays varying amounts of attention to how they prepare their appearance—from the clothes they wear to whether they use deodorant or cologne—in order to create certain impressions on the other. Everything they say and do has the potential to alter or reinforce an impression, from when they choose to laugh to the opinions they express, from the language they use to express themselves to the amount of eye contact they are willing to tolerate, from the food they order to the way they eat it, from who

---

[22] See G. H. Mead, *Mind, Self, and Society* (Chicago: University of Chicago Press, 1934).

[23] Goffman's books make for fascinating reading. See in particular *The Presentation of Self in Everyday Life* (New York: Doubleday, 1959); *Encounters* (Indianapolis: Bobbs-Merrill, 1961); *Asylums* (New York: Anchor Books, 1961); *Behavior in Public Places* (New York: The Free Press, 1963); and *Interaction Ritual* (New York: Anchor Books, 1967).

insists on paying the check to whether either seeks a good night kiss. And at the end of the evening, each is likely to experience a certain amount of wondering—if not anxiety—about how well their performance went and how it may have been interpreted and received by the other.

Goffman's perspective is revealing because like most symbolic interactionists he is trying to discover the mechanisms—the use of language, gestures, and the physical props that contribute to our appearance—through which we create, sustain, and manage our social selves in relation to others, out of which comes what we know as social life among individuals. Goffman interprets embarrassment, for example, as a way of signaling to others that although we may have failed in a particular performance by not meeting expectations, we are nonetheless committed to the legitimacy of those expectations. A display of embarrassment, then, can be viewed as a way of minimizing the threat to our position in the play that might result from a failed performance.[24] Goffman recognizes that we use many techniques to sustain the role performance itself and that the audience has a vested interest in our succeeding, because if we fail, it destabilizes their own performance since all roles exist only in relation to other roles. Thus, there is an interest in sustaining the play, whether it be a family gathering, a meeting of a presidential cabinet, or even a war.

Related to this problem is a branch of the interactionist perspective known as ethnomethodology, which focuses on the social mechanisms—the symbols, gestures, appearance, and behavior—that people use to sustain the shared sense that the social reality we construct in fact exists in some way external to us.[25] It is improbable that people would feel obliged to behave in ways that are defined as appropriate in a particular situation unless they shared a sense that the situation and the expectations that go with it were real. This means, for example, that people will wait their turn in line at a movie theater only if they share a sense that there is such a thing in social life as a line and a set of expectations that

---

[24] See Erving Goffman. "Embarrassment and Social Organization," *American Journal of Sociology*, 62 (1956–1957):264–71.

[25] The founder of ethnomethodology is Harold Garfinkel. See his *Studies in Ethnomethodology* (Englewood Cliffs, NJ: Prentice-Hall, 1967). See also Hugh Mehan and Houston Wood, *The Reality of Ethnomethodology* (New York: John Wiley and Sons, 1975).

are attached to people standing in one. In this sense, people are bound together by the ability to sustain a shared *sense* that social situations exist.

Ethnomethodologists point out that every relationship depends on the assumption that the participants share a common reality, an assumption that must be maintained in order for the relationship to endure. Marriages, for example, typically involve an assumption that each spouse loves the other. One method for maintaining this sense of reality is to engage in rituals such as kissing each other before going to sleep or when parting during the day, or saying "I love you" before ending a telephone conversation. These are far more than perfunctory rituals, which becomes clear when one partner fails to kiss the other or reciprocate an "I love you"—often evoking a sense that something is not quite as it is supposed to be. The shared sense that love is mutual may be shaken. It is in this way, in fact, that ethnomethodologists discover many such mechanisms: they discover rules and implicit understandings by violating them and observing the reaction.

In all of its variations, the interactionist perspective focuses on the interface between people and social systems: the ways in which the abstract ideas contained in roles are in fact manifested in people's appearance and behavior; reality is negotiated and shaped by social actors in relation to one another; and structures emerge from behavior and the symbolic understandings that underlie it. It is a crucial element for us to understand, because it is here that people feel the full weight of social systems, and it is here that social systems become more than abstract ideas in the minds of their participants and the sociologists who study them.

Theory and
Theoretical Perspectives

The functional, conflict, ecological, and interactionist perspectives offer quite different views of social life, but their focus on social systems and people's relationships to them locates them in the common ground defined by the larger sociological framework described in the opening sections of this chapter.

Theoretical perspectives, of course, do not explain anything, but merely establish approaches to explanations, beginning by identifying what needs explaining. A functional approach to the institution of slavery, for example, might raise questions about how slavery is integrated into the operation of major social institutions such as the economy, family, church, and state, and how it affects those systems in both the short and long runs. A conflict perspective would be more concerned with the inequality between slaves and slaveholders and the ways in which control over major social institutions was used to benefit the latter at the expense of the former. An ecological approach might focus on how differences in population, production technology, and the physical environment make slavery more likely in some societies than others. An interactionist perspective might focus on how slavery as an institution is manifested in the day-to-day relationships among those involved—such as the use of gestures and symbols by slaves and owners to create and sustain impressions of themselves. How did slaves, for example, indicate deference to whites regardless of their true feelings, or how did slaveholders reconcile the cruelty of their institutions with their self-images as good Christians?

These statements identify questions about how the institution of slavery works as viewed from different theoretical perspectives, but none actually explains anything, which is precisely what theoretical frameworks are supposed to do. The actual explanations—how legal systems were used in the United States to implement and maintain oppression, how the cultural rhetoric of Christianity was bent to accommodate the realities of slave life, or how different modes of production actually create the conditions in which slavery is more or less likely to emerge as a social institution—all fall within the realm of theory as distinct from theoretical perspectives. Theoretical perspectives provide a general orientation to a problem from which emerge the questions we want to answer. By comparison, theories represent attempts to actually answer particular questions.

Theories arise from perspectives because perspectives define the points of view from which problems are identified and framed. Use of the population-ecological perspective, for example, would likely lead to the finding that slavery is found in only 10 percent of gathering and hunting societies but occurs in 83 percent of advanced horticultural societies.[26] One explanation is that the inability of gathering societies to produce and accumulate surplus wealth makes slavery economically useless, while the ability to produce a surplus in agrarian societies coupled with the labor

---

[26] Lenski and Lenski, op. cit.

intensiveness of agrarian economies makes slavery more attractive economically.

Notice, however, that although this perspective identifies ecological conditions that seem to be *necessary* for slavery to occur, an understanding of why these conditions result in slavery in some cases but not others requires additional factors that go beyond technology and production. If we extend the above line of reasoning, for example, we might conclude that slavery should be most common in industrial societies whose potential to produce and accumulate wealth dwarfs anything that has been seen before. Yet the truth is just the opposite—that slavery is in fact quite rare in industrial societies. Why?

One explanation of this would go beyond the ecological-population perspective to identify cultural and structural characteristics of social systems that have changed along with the mode of production. With industrialization, for example, has come urbanization, the emergence of an educated middle class, and the growth of the mass media—all of which have fostered the development of cultural ideologies and political structures supporting people's rights to determine their own destinies and live free from oppression and exploitation.

What makes the sociological perspective so useful is that it invites us to move among several different dimensions and levels of analysis, to think in ways that span the distance between the largest-scale processes and structures on the one hand and the most intimate informal interactions on the other. It has the potential to take us into the complexity and richness of social systems and, in the process, locate and better understand human life in relation to them.

CHAPTER
SIX

— ◆ —

Thinking and
Living
Sociologically

This book has been about the central importance of how we think, because how we think is deeply bound up with how we perceive, feel, and act. Thinking sociologically is more than an intellectual pursuit, although it certainly can be experienced as such. Learning to think sociologically is also about *living* sociologically, about bringing a critical awareness of culture, social structure, population, and ecology to every social system in which we participate, from our families and work to our countries and the world. It means understanding not only social systems and our positions in them, but also how they become part of us, our sense of who we are, and what our lives are about.

Thinking sociologically can affect people's lives in many ways, but the most important of these touch on three basic issues. The first is an increasing awareness of the implicit understandings and unarticulated assumptions that underlie everyday life with other people. It involves looking beneath the surface of appearance, talk, and behavior to appreciate what is going on at a deeper level. The second involves perceptions of the larger world of social issues and problems—poverty, revolution, war, drug abuse, crime, family violence, homelessness, pollution, abortion, racism, education, injustice, oppression. The third joins the first two by raising questions about our connections as individuals with such issues, how we locate ourselves in relation to social systems and their consequences even though we have had no hand in creating them and have very little control over them.

The following pages will illustrate and go more deeply into each of these by exploring three questions: What does "I love you" really mean? Why are social problems so difficult to solve? and Who are we really?

"I Love You"

Most of us experience language as little more than a means of labeling the world and communicating, of representing to others and ourselves what we perceive, feel, and think. Language, however, is also a social fact that binds social systems together. On the most basic level, language is the symbolic medium through which we both create and represent a shared reality that serves as the basis for social life itself. It is the stuff of which ideas and information are constructed, as well as the shared assumption that those ideas are held in common. Without that assumption cultural ideas would not exist, which means that social systems and social life would not exist.

For all the importance of language as a means of communication, one of its least studied and most intriguing aspects is its use to speak and write as meaningful actions themselves—what is known as performative language.[1] We often use language to describe what we have done, are doing, or expect to do, but this is not understood as the behavior itself; it is merely symbolic. Performative language, however, is not a representation of behavior, but meaningful behavior in its own right. When we say "I

---

[1] See W. P. Robinson, *Language and Social Behavior* (Baltimore, MD: Penguin, 1972).

promise," we do more than communicate a state of mind or set of intentions; we also enter into a socially recognized and binding relationship with others in which we subject ourselves to norms and their sanctions. To say "I promise" *is* to promise. This holds for any kind of oath, from presidential commitments to uphold the principles upon which the nation is built to a courtroom witness swearing to tell the truth.

Probably the best known example of performative language is the "I do" spoken by bride and groom at a wedding. It is no accident that these two simple words are so often a source of humor or anxiety in drama and films as the audience waits breathlessly while a character stands there in silence, holding onto the potential *not* to say them. All of the other words in a marriage ceremony amount to nothing without these two which, when spoken and responded to in kind have the authority to literally transform the relationship between two people and their families, as well as their relationship to social institutions such as the state. What makes this language performative is that its use in the appropriate social situation is essential to change the structure of a relationship. Unlike other uses of language, it does not merely represent reality—it acts upon that reality and becomes part of it.

In the case of the "I do," the changes involved and the role played by language are apparent. But a sociologically more interesting case is the use of performative language in a way that we are generally unaware of. When people say "I'm sorry," for example, they may be simply expressing sorrow for the loss or injury suffered by another, whether caused by them or not. In many cases, however, this phrase is used as performative language to alter a social relationship. When we cause other people injury or loss, we incur a social obligation to accept and endure their anger—if not punishment—and, if possible, to make restitution. As performative language, "I'm sorry" can be used to control this relationship by satisfying the social obligations attached to an offending party. If someone injures you and you become angry, they might say "I'm sorry," and if you persist with your anger, they might reply, "I said I was sorry, didn't I?" In this case they call upon the transforming authority of performative language to nullify the disadvantage resulting from their behavior and the relationship of offender-to-offended that it created.

"I love you" is one of the most powerful bits of hidden performative language. Since the blossoming of romantic love in the age of chivalry, "I love you" has become one of the most important phrases humans hope to hear or utter—at least in Western industrial societies. Literature, film, music, and art all confront us with reflections of what seems to be a collective obsession with interpersonal loving—getting it, having it, keeping it, and adjusting to its loss. There are few things in our lives that have as much command over our sense of well-being and our willingness to take risks and appear foolish as the quest to hear these words.

We could interpret "I love you" as a phrase that communicates information with a high value in our culture. Just as the dance of honeybees indicates to other bees the direction and distance to a newly-discovered supply of nectar, "I love you" conveys a message about how one person perceives and feels about another. If the social function of "I love you" was simply to represent and communicate a set of positive feelings, perceptions, and predispositions, however, then we would expect this phrase to be always welcomed enthusiastically, especially in a society in which people are as fixated (as we seem to be) on loving and being loved. But, of course, as everyone knows from experience, this is not the case, for in many ways it is just as difficult to have the wrong person say "I love you" as it is to have the right person not say it.

Saying "I love you" is problematic because we use language not simply to represent and communicate reality, but to create it as well, especially with performative language. "I love you" can get us into trouble because as performative rather than merely communicative language, it constitutes a social fact with considerable power.

From the perspective of exchange theory, for example, saying "I love you" is a gift of sorts that, in accordance with the norm of reciprocity, requires the recipient to complete the exchange by replying in kind.[2] It could also be interpreted as a gesture of vulnerability and self-exposure, a risk in the name of deepening a relationship that, as with a gift, also carries the expectation of some reciprocity. In either case, it is usually true that when we tell people we love them—especially for the first time—we do so with the hope, if not the expectation, that they will tell us they love us, too, unless, as is true of many long-standing relationships, we are

---

[2] For a more extended and formal treatment of love as exchange, see Peter M. Blau, *Exchange and Power in Social Life* (New York: Wiley, 1964). For more on the norm of reciprocity, see Alvin W. Gouldner, "The Norm of Reciprocity," *American Sociological Review* 25 (April 1960):161–78.

so certain of their feelings that we take reciprocity for granted. Except for this, a reply that falls short—such as "That's wonderful; thank you for sharing that with me" or "It's wonderful that you love me"—is likely to leave us feeling not only dissatisfied, but exposed, vulnerable, even humiliated. Anyone who has taken this kind of initiative knows the agony of waiting for the hoped-for response; and anyone who has been on the receiving end without wanting to be knows the awkwardness of feeling obliged to reciprocate.

But, we might ask, why not just fake a response if need be to satisfy the norm of reciprocity (as in "You look great." "So do you.")? Although people certainly could and sometimes actually do this, they have to ignore (at their peril) that "I love you" has a much deeper meaning as performative language, whose significance goes considerably beyond simple exchange. In situations with romantic potential (as distinct from parent and child, for example), that first utterance of "I love you" is far more than an expression of perception, feelings, or predisposition intended to make someone feel good; it is also an invitation and expression of intent to alter a social relationship. If we reciprocate with "I love you, too," the social rights, expectations, and obligations that connect us can change dramatically. Henceforth, we might be expected to add sexuality to our relationship, to value each other more than anyone else, to prefer each other's company, to confide in and be loyal to each other, especially sexually, and even to form a permanent relationship such as marriage. As performative language, the words do more than communicate; they constitute meaningful acts that signify a transformation not of us as individuals, but of the relationship between us. It is, in short, "I do" on a less binding level and is important less for what it means than for what it does. In this sense, all of the positive messages one might read into "I love you" are, without the words themselves, only information without transformation: "You say you think I'm wonderful, beautiful, sexy, smart, and funny, that I excite you, interest you, attract you, and move you, that you want to be with me; but you've never said you love me."

Loving and the performative language that surrounds it is more than feeling or behavior; it is also a role relationship that, like any other, is subject to various forms of social control. The words are crucial because they regulate the structural boundaries which must be crossed in order to become lovers with another, and for this reason we do well to be careful when and with whom we use them. Note in this connection how important the use of the subject "I" and the verb "love" are in making the language performative. Many people use the word love—as when signing a letter to a friend—who might never say "I love you" to that same person. The difference can be that between expressing a sentiment on the one hand and substantially altering a relationship on the other. Although the former can have performative effects, they are so to a much smaller degree.

Having crossed the boundary demarcated by "I love you," we may feel we have not only obligations to, but also some measure of power over, another. This difference between love as feeling and love as role relationship is beautifully illustrated in the cult classic film, *Harold and Maude*, in which a young and suicidal Harold meets and falls in love with the elderly free spirit Maude. On her seventieth birthday Maude takes a drug overdose in a long-planned suicide based on her reckoning for herself when she would be ready to die. When Maude tells Harold what she has done, he protests that she can't do this because "I love you, Maude." But she does not join him in his definition of feeling as relationship: "Wonderful!" she replies, "Go love some more!"

Because performative language has the cultural authority to transform relationships, it can also be used to manipulate the definition of social situations. We can say "I love you" to someone knowing that this will alter their expectations and feelings of obligation to us without sharing those expectations and feelings ourselves. This amounts to a form of social fraud in which the stakes can be both material and emotional. When a man falsely tells a woman that he loves her to create a situation that she requires in order to have sexual intercourse, he uses performative language fraudulently. Similarly, performative language can sustain existing relationships. Just as married couples sometimes repeat their marriage ceremony to reaffirm their vows, so too, couples often use "I love you" to reinforce their relationship on a less formal, ceremonial level. In some cases, "I love you" is used as performative language to conceal that the underlying message of how we perceive and feel about someone no longer applies, as when people say "I love you" to sustain a relationship long after they cease feeling or behaving in a loving way. Batterers are well known for apologizing to battered spouses and invoking the words "I love you" as a way of denying the reality of their abusive behavior and, in many cases, the performative language is powerful enough to overcome what victims know to be the truth.

It is important to note that "I love you" is used as performative language in many contexts other than romantic relationships, with quite different dynamics and results. When parents say "I love you" to their children, it has a very different meaning than when spoken by children to their parents, for parent and child roles are not equivalent. For the parent, the words can express loving sentiments (as well as obscure abuse), but more importantly they convey a commitment to the child's well-being. So central is this commitment to the role of parent that the language of love used to convey it may have little to do with positive feelings for children (which is why children often distinguish between "I love you" and "I like you," with the latter viewed as more important for self-esteem, especially during adolescence when such issues become crucial). For children—especially when they are old enough to speak the words but too young to have any real understanding of their meaning—"I love you" may be less an expression of their own positive regard for their parents as people than a learned way of eliciting reassurance from their parents. There are, of course, parents who reverse this manipulation by looking to even young children to support them emotionally and who may use "I love you" to elicit a corresponding sign of commitment to the parent's well-being. A related version of this is the parent who uses, "I love you" as a way of inducing guilt and, with it, compliance.

The power of performative language calls upon us to use it with care unless we want to risk provoking the scorn reserved for people who use it with too little respect for its cultural authority. Nothing renders someone so unfit for social relationships as the repeated abuse of performative language—the person who lies, who breaks promises, who dodges responsibility for injury and loss, or who professes love falsely or even casually.

Language is far more than talk and we in using it, are more than mere talkers. We are creators and transformers, spinning the social world as we speak.

Putting the "Social"
Back Into Social Problems

Reading the daily newspaper and seeing the many problems that face modern societies such as the United States, it is difficult to avoid the impression that nothing seems to work. Governments and their programs come and go, as do debates between opposing political parties, but the problems remain and, if anything, grow worse along with people's feelings of collective frustration and despair.

It is fair to say that the problems are not solved partly because they are so broad in scope and complexity. But sociologists are drawn to a deeper explanation too often overlooked and rarely examined in a critical way: solving social problems requires that first they be understood as *social* problems with causes or consequences that are characteristics of social systems. Consider, for example, the case of poverty, perhaps the most far-reaching, long-standing, and devastating social problem of them all. Given the enormous wealth produced in the United States, the level of poverty and near-poverty is quite high, especially among non-whites, in spite of the sizable dent made by the 1960s federal "War on Poverty." Roughly 15 percent of the population lives below the poverty level, and if we include the near-poor, the percentage rises easily to 20 percent or more. Among children, the poor and near-poor include one out of every four.[3] Even the middle class is increasingly insecure, as the cost of buying a house or paying for college education escalates beyond the means of most families, even when both parents work.

How do we explain such levels of poverty and financial insecurity in the midst of an abundant wealth unprecedented in human history? From a sociological perspective, the distribution of wealth and income is a structural characteristic of social systems, and as such, can be understood as a consequence of those systems.[4] As a capitalist society, for example, the United States allows a minority to control most capital, forcing the working majority to live on wages. This facilitates the accumulation of wealth, with a small elite controlling the vast majority of wealth and income, and leaving a relatively small portion for the rest of the population. With a majority of the population competing for a disproportionately small share of the resources, a portion of that population will inevitably come up short and live in poverty. Part of the cause of poverty, then, lies in the nature of an economic

---

[3] U.S. Census Bureau, *Statistical Abstract of the United States, 1990.* (Washington, DC: U.S. Government Printing Office, 1990), Table 745.

[4] See Richard C. Edwards, Michael Reich, and Thomas E. Weisskopf, eds., *The Capitalist System: A Radical Analysis of American Society* (Englewood Cliffs, NJ: Prentice-Hall, 1986); Michael Harrington, *The New American Poverty* (New York: Penguin, 1985); and Harold R. Kerbo, *Social Stratification and Inequality: Class Conflict in the United States,* 2nd ed. (New York: McGraw-Hill, 1991).

system that facilitates and encourages the accumulation and concentration of wealth.

The level of poverty is also linked to basic ways in which industrial capitalism operates as a social system. The primary importance that capitalism places on competition, efficiency, and profit, for example, encourages control over costs by keeping wages low, the use of machines to replace workers, the introduction of high technology that renders obsolete the less sophisticated skills of many workers, moving jobs to locations where labor is cheaper and more easily managed (especially to Third World countries), and closing operations whose level of profit is insufficient to retain the interest of investors looking for a maximum return on their funds. These imperatives arise from the normal operation of capitalism as an economic system, and they result in dislocation, anxiety, and hardship for millions of workers. Even those employed full time often find that capitalist competition between firms forces wages so low that their families fall near or below the poverty line.

To these social factors we can add others, such as government policies that increase interest rates — resulting in higher unemployment — to fight inflation; the high divorce rate and the corresponding increase in single-parent families; the inevitable business cycle of boom and recession that throws people out of work without picking them all up again when the economy swings upward; the centuries-old legacies of racism in the form of poor education, despair, prejudice, and discrimination; and the simple fact that the vast majority of people own no productive property and, as such, have little direct control over any means of making a living other than to make themselves attractive in a changing job market.

Although these are by no means offered as a last word on the causes of poverty, this discussion illustrates how poverty in a society can be understood as a consequence produced by that society. At the level of collective action and understanding, however, relatively little use is made of this kind of analysis in the U.S. Instead, most approaches to poverty take one of two basic forms, perhaps best described as liberal and conservative. A perfect example of the conservative approach is found in Charles Murray's book *Losing Ground*, which spoke for many conservatives during the Reagan administration.[5] Murray argued that the world

---

[5] New York: Basic Books, 1984.

is like a merry-go-round on which the goal is to make sure that "everyone has a reasonably equal chance at the brass ring—or at least a reasonably equal chance to get on the merry-go-round."[6] After reviewing thirty years of federal programs intended to eliminate poverty, Murray concluded the failure of these policies indicates that individual initiative and effort lie at the core of both the causes of poverty and any successful attempt to eliminate it. He would do away with affirmative action programs as well as all federal welfare and income-support systems, including

> AFDC, Medicaid, food stamps, unemployment insurance, and the rest. It would leave the working-aged person with no recourse whatsoever except the job market, family members, friends, and public or private locally funded services.[7]

The result, he argued, would "make it possible to get as far as one can go on one's merit."[8]

Although the U.S. has not adopted the kind of draconian measures Murray prescribes, his argument touches a deep nerve in the nation's cultural consciousness. There is widespread acceptance of his view of society and the causes of inequality, yet at the same time there is little support for the kinds of policies they would lead to. The belief that individuals are basically responsible for their own outcomes, for example, has not led to a widespread demand to eradicate programs that benefit the needy. One explanation for this inconsistency between belief and action is that although Murray's views resonate with the ideology of individualism that is so powerful in the United States, there is the nagging but largely unarticulated recognition that it does not tell the whole story. This conflict rests on a basic confusion between two very different aspects of social inequality in general and poverty in particular.

On the one hand is the question of how individuals are sorted into different social class categories—the kind of question that is the focus of most sociological research on social mobility and status attainment: What individual characteristics best predict occupation and income? Who gets ahead? These are questions people are most familiar with because they reflect their own attempts to make the most of their lives. Although it may seem counterintuitive, however, these kinds of questions have relatively little to do with

---

[6] Ibid., p. 221.

[7] Ibid., pp. 227–28.

[8] Ibid., p. 233.

the larger questions of why inequality in general and poverty in particular exist and persist.

Imagine that income is distributed according to the outcome of a footrace. All of the income for a year is put in a pool from which people draw according to their place: the first fifth of the field splits 45 percent of the pool, the second fifth wins 25 percent, the third fifth gets 16 percent, the fourth splits fifth 10 percent, and the last fifth collects just 4 percent. The result of such a system would be an unequal distribution of income with roughly the apportionment by population fifths found in the United States.

If we then ask, "Why is there inequality; why is there so much poverty?" one obvious answer—and, to many, the only answer— is that some people get more because they run faster. If we want to explain why two people have different or similar outcomes, this explanation would suffice, although we would probably ask why some people can run faster than others. But if we want to understand why one-fifth must survive on only 4 percent of the income, the answer that they are the slowest runners is inade- quate, for this ignores the terms of the race itself that require *some* fifth of the population to live in poverty. If the prize money were distributed more evenly by fifths, there would be less poverty regardless of how fast people could run.[9]

There are two very different phenomena involved here. On the one hand are the choices and abilities that affect how well people can live: going to college, for example, tends to have a positive effect on income. On the other hand are the limitations social systems impose which produce patterns of inequality among individuals regardless of what they do: the cost of college places it beyond the reach of most, and given a limited number of well-paid jobs for college graduates, even those who earn degrees may find themselves unemployed or working in jobs far below their training and abilities. To the extent that we confuse the former with the latter (by reducing the race and its outcome to the ability and behavior of the runners) we conceal the social dynamics that produce social problems. In the U.S., this tendency is so entrenched that even those who think they are attributing social problems to social causes often wind up attributing them to individuals instead.

---

[9] If, for example, the first fifth split 22 percent, the second 21 percent, the third 20 percent, the fourth 19 percent, and the fifth 18 percent, there would still be inequality, but since the share going to the top and bottom fifths would be very close to what would be an equal share of the total pot, the system would allow for far fewer extremes of wealth and poverty.

This can be seen both in Murray's analysis and in the responses of many of his critics. Murray's greatest mistake lies not in this selective reading of the data on poverty and federal programs but with his conclusion that if poverty persists in spite of federal antipoverty programs, then the causes of poverty must lie with individuals and their responses to reward and punishment, not with social systems. But the failure of such programs cannot be used to reject the idea that social systems produce poverty because these programs were not grounded in a sociological analysis of the causes of inequality and poverty to begin with. Even liberals, who are most likely to attribute poverty to social causes, focus on what amounts to a slightly more complex version of individualism. By "social," they seem to mean that problems affect many people or that social institutions have some responsibility to do something, but this is a far cry from understanding how systems produce the problem in the first place. Governmental programs have failed not because the idea that poverty is produced by social systems is incorrect, but because policymakers have not understood the meaning of that idea or, therefore, how to act on it. Like most people in the U.S., both liberals and conservatives have not known how to get beyond individualistic, personal achievement models of social inequality.

This inability is very much in evidence in the two major types of antipoverty programs. The first, best exemplified by job training and other educational programs, holds individuals ultimately responsible for social inequality by assuming that the distribution of poverty and wealth result solely from differences in qualifications and behavior. The only new twist introduced by these programs is that social institutions are taking some responsibility for changing the distribution of individual ability and motivation. To return to the analogy of the footrace, this amounts to making physical training more widely available, but without changing the rules of the race that produce the patterns of inequality by attaching different outcomes to where one happens to finish. The result is a certain amount of reshuffling of individuals among the different fifths, but without changing the overall distribution of outcomes, since the standards will still ensure that a certain proportion will be poor.

The second type of program assumes that social systems produce inequality and poverty, but is justified as humanitarian compassion for the victims. In either case, instead of changing the social systems that produce inequality and poverty, these programs try to compensate for their negative consequences. This category includes all welfare and income-transfer programs, from unemployment compensation and food stamps to Medicaid and subsidized housing. There is much to recommend them since they alleviate some harmful consequences, but in the long run they do little to alter the scope of poverty in the society as a whole. This approach is analogous to the doctor whose patient is bleeding to death, and who gives one transfusion after another without locating or repairing the wound. Murray's position amounts to arguing that transfusions just throw good blood after bad, and in the long run, he may be correct. But if he is right, it is for the wrong reasons, since his alternative—leaving patients to their own devices to avoid an unhealthy dependency—makes it no more likely that the source of the bleeding will be identified, much less healed. He simply shifts the responsibility for the loss of blood elsewhere.

Attempts to solve social problems have often rested on an individualistic approach to social life cloaked in pseudosociological terms, which is to say, they reflect a profound misunderstanding of what makes social problems "social." It is a very narrow view to argue that society is responsible for social problems only in the sense that institutions have a general humanitarian obligation to assist those who suffer as a result. And that view is broadened only slightly by including the responsibility to assist individuals as they struggle not to be the ones who must finish last in the race (which, inevitably, leaves that position to others so long as the social system is structured as it is). Insofar as social problems are more than an accumulation of individual woes, solutions will be found only among the workings of social systems themselves. It will mean raising difficult critical questions about major social institutions, from corporate capitalism and politics to education and the family. It will mean considering the possibility that industrial capitalism may be fundamentally incompatible with the idea of a just society. It will mean seeing schools as more than a means to upward mobility, as institutions in which class, gender, and racial inequality is reproduced in each generation. Putting the "social" back into our approach to social problems promises to be an arduous and at times even frightening process; but it is most likely the only way these problems will ever be solved.

Who Are We Really?

On a cool spring evening some years ago I took a walk down the street I lived on in a small university town. Darkness was just coming on and there were few other people on the street. As I walked I approached a young woman walking in the opposite direction. Although I had never seen her before, as we grew near I sensed something in her that startled and perplexed me and, as my vivid memory of it attests, still troubles me almost twenty years later. When we passed each other, she dropped her head, averted her eyes, quickened her step, and veered just a little to one side to widen the gap between us. The feeling of fear that she projected was in unmistakable and stark contrast to the tranquillity of this place and what I knew to be my own benign feelings and intentions.

I suspect that her reaction had nothing to do with my feelings or intentions, but only my visible membership in a social category—adult male—that has a propensity for violence against women. Knowing nothing about me except for that, she treated me with a demeanor bordering on fearful deference. That this was a response I did not want seemed beside the point—which is precisely the sociological point. Among the consequences of social systems are patterns of perception, feeling, thought, and behavior that are, to a considerable degree, independent of what each of us intends. That I am not violent with women or anyone else is in this case sociologically irrelevant, for the power associated with the category of adult male is based on larger social patterns in which I only participate. She, of course, was also on one level participating in larger social systems as the occupant of the status of adult female, and the odds that she would be victimized by sexual violence (assuming she had not been already) would depend more than anything on her status, not the details of her personal desires and intentions. In other words, being male can be enough to invoke fear because being female can be enough to identify a potential victim of male aggression and sexual violence.[10]

My sense is that many people experience a lot of confusion about their connection as individuals to the social categories of

---

[10] There is a growing literature on sexual violence. See, in particular, Susan Brownmiller, *Against Our Will* (New York: Simon and Schuster, 1975), and A. Medea and K. Thompson, *Against Rape* (New York: Farrar, Straus, and Giroux, 1974). Probably the foremost sociologist working in this area is Diana Russell. See, for example, *Rape in Marriage* (New York: Macmillan, 1982); *Sexual Exploitation* (Beverly Hills, CA: Sage, 1984); and *The Secret Trauma: Incest in the Lives of Girls and Women* (New York: Basic Books, 1986).

gender, and considerable ambivalence about what that connection means. In spite of the women's movement, for example, many women deny that anything other than their personal attributes affect their outcomes in life. This seems to be particularly true of younger women who have had relatively little adult experience of work and family life, and whose denial of the importance of gender politics also denies that their gender is a major linkage between them and social systems. It is almost as if they believe that gender does not exist as a social category, only as a socially insignificant characteristic like eye color.

This split between the personal and the social runs even deeper among men whose identity as men in a male-dominated society makes them especially vulnerable to feelings of responsibility and guilt. Judging from the writings associated with the men's movement, for example, many seem to feel that women blame them as individuals and hold them personally accountable for the dominance of men as a social category and masculinity as its cultural basis. Since none of these men invented patriarchy as a social system, and since many identify themselves as sympathetic to the goals of the women's movement, they are troubled by the ways in which they are identified personally with a status they happen to occupy through accident of birth.

This dilemma is not confined to gender, for people born and socialized into dominant positions in social systems they did not create are always vulnerable to feeling a sense of guilt associated with their position. Many whites, for example, struggle with questions of personal guilt about centuries-old patterns of race relations that place them in a privileged racial category. In similar ways, many Germans who were not even born at the time of Nazi rule must contend with issues of guilt and responsibility arising simply from being German. Once again, on the other side of these issues are categories of people such as blacks and Jews who were and still are victimized by dominant groups simply because they occupy minority statuses. For them, too, there are difficult issues that arise from their connection to those categories, from the one extreme of so completely identifying themselves with their minority-defining status that they otherwise disappear as individuals, to the other extreme of denying that race, ethnicity, and religion have any social significance at all.

As the gaps between the haves and have-nots increase both within and between societies, our connections with categories of social class and nationality also become problematic. When middle- and upper-class Americans pass homeless people on the streets of cities and towns, part of the discomfort they often feel is undoubtedly rooted in the knowledge that their appearance identifies them as among those who have homes and the other basic necessities of life. When they refuse a request for money, they do so knowing that although the person they refuse knows nothing about them personally, they do have some idea of the socioeconomic category they fall in and the knowledge that the refusal is not based on a sheer inability to give some amount of spare change. People cannot, in short, conceal cultural indicators of class position or avoid being perceived and judged according to them.

When U.S. tourists travel in Third World countries, the situation is more complex because both class and nationality differences are involved. In Mexico, for example, poverty is so pervasive and poor people so visible that tourists cannot avoid encountering them every day, many reaching out for money. In such encounters it is difficult to avoid the awareness that beggars—many of them children—can identify Americans simply on sight and from this construct beliefs and expectations that may not apply to Americans as individuals at all. For those familiar with the history of relations between the United States and countries such as Mexico, it is also difficult not to feel that as Americans they represent that history and bear some responsibility for its consequences. In short, class and nationality are not simply objective characteristics that identify material resources and place of birth; they are meaningful categories in systems of relations and as such they indicate to others the aspects of social identities which we may or may not want to include in our personal views of who we are.

Although we might question who we are in relation to every status we occupy, the issues are especially difficult concerning statuses used to assign rights and privileges in stratified societies (and in a stratified world). In general, those who are conscious of their disadvantaged social position are most likely to be aware of the importance of social categories and to embrace them as important parts of their social identities. Those who find themselves in privileged positions, however, often dissociate themselves from statuses such as race, gender, and religion as part of the denial that their advantages flow from anything other than their own merit and effort (although they may embrace upper-class membership since the legitimacy of upper-class dominance and privilege have not been challenged in the way that race, gender, ethnicity, and religion have). White men who complain about affirmative action programs designed to benefit blacks and women tend to be aware of their own talents and hard work but unaware of their social advantages over blacks and women who are just as talented and work just as hard as they do. They are largely unaware or deny that their own success depended in part on limitations on competition created through barriers routinely placed in front of women and blacks, including the general absence of positive cultural imagery and role models, encouragement and support in school, and outright discrimination. When they do identify with their advantageous statuses, it often has less to do with the privileges conferred by the workings of the social system than with the supposedly superior qualifications of those who occupy those statuses. In other words, a man may attribute part of his success to his gender, but only in the sense that he believes that his gender actually does confer some measure of inherent superiority on him.

These issues derive from the much broader sociological insight that although we are more than status occupants who perform roles, we cannot separate ourselves from our statuses. From the moment we are born—if not before—everything we are and experience is so entwined with social systems that it is simply not possible to disentangle completely the personal from the social without resorting to some real intellectual hocus pocus. What is missing for many people is a sense of balance in their perception of themselves as individuals on the one hand and status occupants on the other.

This touches on the fundamental sociological problem that has to do with the nature of interaction in general and the connection of individuals to social systems in particular. As we saw in Chapter 5, we can think of structure and culture as independent of individuals, with their own characteristics and dynamics. According to this view, networks of statuses and roles and the social systems they comprise are distinct from the people who participate in them. However, people are far more than status occupants passively enacting the patterns that inhere in role relationships. As interactionists make clear, our experience and behavior are the result of an active interpretation of other people's behavior and the social systems in which it occurs. We are creative beings who continually affect the structures and shared understandings of social life.[11]

One analytical problem that emerges from these views is seeing clearly how these two dimensions intersect—just what individuals and social systems have to do with each other. Although this is a basic problem in sociology, it is also a personal problem that we contend with in the continuing process of creating and sustaining a stable sense of who we are and what our lives are about. Social statuses and social systems cannot be reduced to individuals just as individuals cannot be reduced to the statuses they occupy. And yet our lives are deeply involved with those statuses and there are many occasions when we must wrestle with questions of personal identity in light of them, of how we perceive and experience and, sometimes, judge ourselves in the context of our statuses and the roles associated with them.

A lack of clarity about our relation to social statuses can raise difficult issues about our feelings of authenticity. Especially in individualistic societies such as the United States, people tend to view the social self—the occupant of social statuses who performs a multiplicity of roles—as inherently less authentic than what is envisioned as an underlying real self. Roles are played or performed and are, therefore, like masks that hide some real underlying "us" just as theatrical roles conceal the actors who play them. But this view requires separating the two notions of self not only analytically, but to some degree in our actual experience of ourselves, as if each of us is split into different selves and, apart from all of these, a real self.

Splitting ourselves, however, into many different selves with varying degrees of reality deprives us of an overall sense of integration and wholeness. It encourages us to deny responsibility for our behavior by attributing it to vague and unnamed external

---

[11] Among symbolic interactionists there is a continuing debate about the connection between social structure and the behavior of individuals. A polar position is represented by Herbert Blumer, who argues that social structures *are* no more than the creation of actors and their behavior. Critics of Blumer attach greater importance to the external structural constraints exerted on individuals. See Herbert Blumer, *Symbolic Interactionism: Perspective and Method* (Englewood Cliffs, NJ: Prentice-Hall, 1966); Bernard Meltzer and Jerome Petras, "The Chicago and Iowa Schools of Symbolic Interactionism," in T. Shibutani, ed., *Human Nature and Collective Behavior* (Englewood Cliffs, NJ: Prentice-Hall, 1970); and Stanford M. Lyman and Arthur J. Vidich, *Social Order and the Public Philosophy: An Analysis and Interpretation of the Work of Herbert Blumer* (Fayetteville: University of Arkansas Press, 1988).

forces, and, in the process, it costs us much of our power as human beings as well. Whenever we dissociate ourselves from our role behavior, we undermine the reality of our own existence as people with the power to act and have an effect.

An alternative is to integrate ideas about our various selves into the singular view that we are always our real selves. If you play a role that seems to contradict who you think you are, the player is nonetheless yourself and as such is no less real than the "me" who thinks thoughts about the "real me." If you fake it, the impression that results may not match the ideas about yourself that you or others have, but it is the real you who fakes, who manipulates your appearance in order to create that impression. If there is an unreality, it is our tendency to live without an awareness of how we behave, the impressions we create, and the consequences that result (and yet, even this is another aspect of ourselves). As such, the problem lies not so much with performing, but with failing to embrace and admit our performances for what they are. It is not so much the multiplicity of roles that we perform that creates the problems of authenticity, but our failure to integrate them with awareness into our experience of ourselves.

What we so often experience as a problem of authenticity may in fact be a failure to fully appreciate the complicated connection between our internal experience of ourselves and our participation in social systems. And since each of us occupies many different statuses, whenever we interact, portions of ourselves overlap with portions of other selves as statuses are aligned, roles evoked, and we, drawing upon all of the factors that make us who we are, perceive, interpret, feel, and act.

If I was correct in my perception of how that young woman felt when we passed each other on the street years ago, then her fear was based on a social reality—my status as a man in relation to her status as a woman in a particular social system—that did not correspond in important ways with the ideas I have about myself. But this does not mean that her behavior was based on something unreal, for my status as a male adult socially marks me in ways that are quite real in their effects on other people and myself. The relationship between men and women in male-dominated societies is a social fact that touches everyone. It is an aspect of reality which we did not create and over which we may have relatively little control as individuals. But in the social world, it is, whether we like it or not, part of who we really are.

By developing the ability to think in a sociological way, we have the potential to vastly complicate and enrich our own lives, to deepen our understanding not only of the world, but of ourselves. But what is of much greater sociological importance is the potential for change that would emerge if sociological thinking became a pervasive part of any culture, if the collective ability to think critically about how social systems work became a routine part of how they work. We need not envision a world dominated by scientifically based sociological engineering—that is neither possible nor desirable. But we may imagine a world in which people are far better prepared to take collective responsibility for institutions and the consequences they produce, to feel a deeper and clearer sense of connection between their own lives and choices on the one hand and the social systems in which they participate on the other. The world could not help but be better for it.

GLOSSARY

— ◆ —

Achieved status   A status entered after birth and usually due at least in part to individual behavior.

Acquired status   (See **Achieved status**.)

Age structure   The relative number of people of each age in a population.

Agrarian society   A society in which agriculture is the primary means of subsistence.

Alienation   The psychological condition in which individuals feel detached from work, social relationships, and the results of their own behavior.

Anomie   A social condition in which members of groups, communities, or societies no longer feel allegiance to norms.

Anthropology   The study of culture in small, preindustrial societies.

Ascribed status   A status assigned at birth.

Attitudes   Positive or negative evaluations of people, objects, or situations that often predispose people to feel and behave positively or negatively toward them.

Authority   Power assigned according to norms and generally accepted as legitimate by those over whom it is exercised.

Beliefs   Statements about what is real.

Birth cohort   People who share the same year of birth.

Birth rate   The number of children born each year for every thousand members of a population.

Boundary   The specification of who may occupy a particular status. The **clarity** of boundaries describes how easily people can tell who occupies a status. The **openness** of boundaries refers to how easy it is for individuals to occupy a particular status.

Bureaucracy   A complex set of formal, secondary relationships in which (1) entry into statuses is controlled by rigid norms; (2) people specialize in narrowly-defined tasks; (3) roles are rigidly defined by rules; (4) power is distributed in a clear hierarchy; (5)

managers specialize in making sure everything works according to the rules; and (6) decisions are based on rational considerations of the organization's best interests rather than on personal feelings of individuals.

Capital   Means of production whose owners pay workers' wages to produce wealth.

Capitalism   An economic system in which the means of production are privately owned and controlled by those who employ others for wages.

Caste   In stratification systems, a social category in which membership depends on ascribed statuses and cannot be changed.

Charismatic authority   Authority based on the belief that a particular individual possesses special abilities or characteristics.

Class consciousness   An awareness among members of a social class of the true extent and social causes of inequality in a society.

Cohort effect   Effects on people's lives that arise from the characteristics of the historical periods during which they experienced stages of life such as childhood or middle age.

Colonialism   The relationship between countries in which one dominates the other and exploits its natural and human resources.

Commodity   A good or service produced primarily for its exchange value, not for direct consumption by the producer.

Communal economy   An economy based on collective ownership of means of production, primary ties, and sharing.

Communication structure   The frequency and duration of interaction among members of a group.

Communism   A utopian economic system in which the means of production are communally owned and there is no state.

Compound family   A nuclear family in which children are directly related to only one of the parents.

Compound status   A status that consists of one or more statuses joined together as one—as "policewoman" joins occupation with gender.

Conflict perspective   A theoretical perspective that focuses on the struggle among different social groups over scarce rewards.

Conspicuous consumption   Consumption intended to affirm or enhance an individual's prestige.

Core society   In world-system theory, a society that is in an economically dominant position.

Crude birth rate   (See **Birth rate**.)

Crude death rate   (See **Death rate**.)

Cultural relativism   A concept that refers to the fact that the importance of a particular cultural idea varies from one society or subgroup to another.

Cultural universal   A cultural product found in all societies.

Culture   The accumulated sum of symbols, ideas, and material products associated with life in a social system.

Death rate   The number of people who die in a given year for every thousand people in a population.

Definition of the situation   The determination of which statuses and roles are relevant in a social situation.

Demographic transition theory   A theory describing the pattern of falling death and birth rates that has characterized the recent history of industrialized countries.

Demography   The study of the size, composition, growth, and distribution of human populations.

Division of labor   The allocation of different roles among the members of a social system.

Dramaturgy (dramaturgical approach)   The study of social interaction as theater in which actors play roles before audiences.

Dysfunction   The interference of a cultural idea or social structure with the maintenance or adaptation of a social system.

Ecological succession   The process through which ecosystems change.

Ecology   The study of the relationship between populations and their physical environments, including the ability to use natural resources and technology.

Ecosystem   All forms of life that live in relation to one another and a shared physical environment.

Epidemiology   The study of where diseases come from, how they are distributed geographically and socially, and how they are transmitted from one place or person to another.

Ethnic group   A set of people who identify with a common cultural heritage.

Ethnocentrism   The tendency of people to regard the ideas and practices of other cultures as incorrect, if not inferior.

Ethnomethodology   The study of the unspoken rules and meanings through which people sustain the shared belief that social systems exist.

False consciousness   A state of unawareness of, or misperception of, social conditions and their causes, especially when applied to social stratification.

Folkways   The set of manners and customary acts that characterize everyday life in a society.

Function   A contribution of a cultural idea or social structure to the maintenance and adaptation of a social system.

Functional perspective   A theoretical perspective that focuses on the ways in which cultural ideas and social structures contribute to or interfere with the maintenance or adaptation of a social system.

Gatherer-hunter society   A society in which subsistence needs are met primarily by hunting wild game and gathering existing vegetation.

Generalized other   Our perception of the expectations that generally apply to people in a particular social situation.

Gesture   An action that has symbolic meaning.

Group   Two or more people who interact with each other in patterned ways and are identified as members.

Horticultural society   A society in which subsistence needs are met primarily through cultivation of small gardens, but without the use of the plow.

I   Mead's concept that refers to that part of us that directly experiences ourselves and others.

Ideal self   Our image of ourselves as we believe we ought to be.

Ideal type   A concept that describes a "pure" type that does not actually exist.

Ideology   A set of interrelated beliefs, values, attitudes, and norms that are used to explain and/or justify existing social relationships.

Infant mortality rate   The number of infants under the age of one who die in a given year for every 1,000 births that occur during that year.

In-group   A group to which we belong and in which we share a sense of "we-ness" that often excludes and devalues members of other groups.

Institution   An enduring set of cultural ideas and social relationships designed to accomplish one or more goals.

Interactionist perspective   A major theoretical perspective that focuses on the causes and consequences of social behavior, based on the importance of assigning meaning to appearance, behavior, and experience.

Isolation   The degree to which groups do not share the same communities.

Kin   People who are bound together by ties of ancestry, adoption, or marriage.

Kinship   Social relationships that are based on common ancestry, adoption, or marriage.

Labor power   The potential to produce goods — usually measured in terms of time — which workers sell to employers in return for wages.

Legal-rational authority   Power that is based on culturally defined rules that regulate social interaction.

Life expectancy   The average number of remaining years people can expect to live if current death rates remain unchanged throughout their lifetime.

Looking-glass self   Our perception of how other people perceive and evaluate us.

Material culture   Objects made by people as they interact with one another and the physical world.

Me   Mead's concept that refers to the part of the self that looks upon the self as an object.

Microecology   The study of how the number of people involved in a social situation and their physical arrangement in relation to one another affect social interaction.

Mind   The ability to use symbols in order to understand other people's thoughts, feelings, and expectations.

Minority (group)   A collection of people who, because of physical or cultural characteristics, are singled out from others for differential and unequal treatment.

Mode of production The way in which a society goes about producing goods and services, consisting of the means and relations of production.

Modernization A concept describing a process through which societies are believed to change from less to more developed forms through the introduction of new technology and other social change.

Mores The set of deeply held ideas about how people ought to behave.

Niche The position a species of life occupies in an ecosystem.

Nonmaterial culture The products of collective human activity that have no physical reality, including symbols, language, music, beliefs, values, norms, and attitudes.

Norm A rule that attaches sanctions to the behavior or appearance of status occupants.

Opportunity structure The distribution of opportunities to achieve goals.

Out-group A group toward which hostile attitudes are directed by members of another group.

Performative language A meaningful utterance that alters people's positions in social relationships.

Peripheral society In world-system theory, a society that is in an economically subordinate position.

Population A collection of people who share a geographic territory. In research, any precisely defined set of objects, people, groups, or societies.

Postindustrial society A society in which the production of goods is overshadowed by the provision of services, and in which relations between people and machines are gradually replaced by relationships between people.

Power The potential to have an effect on ourselves, others, or our environment.

Power structure The distribution of power among members of groups, organizations, communities, or societies.

Prejudice A positive or negative attitude directed toward people simply because they occupy a status.

Primary relationship A social relationship that exists for its own sake, endures through time, and involves people in many aspects of each other's lives.

Proletariat   In Marx's framework, the working class, which neither owns nor controls any means of production.

Rate of natural increase   The difference between birth and death rates in a population.

Relations of production.   The social relationships through which goods or services are produced.

Role   A set of beliefs, values, norms, and attitudes shared by status occupants in their relationships with the occupants of other statuses.

Role set   A set of roles attached to a single status.

Role structure   The set of roles performed by members of a group.

Sanction   A social punishment or reward associated with obeying or violating a norm.

Secondary relationship   A relationship that is limited to goals that, once achieved, usually end a person's involvement.

Self-concept   The sum total of our thoughts and feelings about ourselves.

Self-esteem   The positive and negative feelings people feel toward themselves.

Self-fulfilling prophecy   A belief that becomes true because we think and act as if it were.

Semiperipheral society   In world-system theory, a society that is in the process of industrializing.

Significant other   A particular individual whose beliefs, evaluations, attitudes, and expectations affect our appearance or behavior.

Situational status   A status occupied only in a particular social situation.

Social category   Two or more people who have a social status in common, but who do not interact in patterned ways.

Social fact   A cultural or structural characteristic of a social system that has constraining effects on people who participate in it.

Social identity   The sum total of who we think we are in relation to other people.

Socialism   An economic arrangement in which the means of production are owned and controlled by the state, not by private individuals or groups.

Socialization   The process through which people learn to think, feel, evaluate, and behave as individuals in relation to social and physical environments.

Social status   A position in a social relationship, a characteristic that locates individuals in relation to other people and sets of role expectations.

Social stratification   The systematic, uneven distribution of valued products of social life such as wealth, power, and prestige among the occupants of different social statuses.

Social structure   The arrangement of people in relation to one another and the patterns of expectation attached to positions in social relationships. Also patterns of expectation between groups, the distribution of people among various social positions, and the distribution of social rewards.

Social system   Any arrangement of social relationships that functions as a whole and can be thought of as a unit.

Society   A population whose members share a cultural identity and way of life, interact in patterned ways, and occupy common geographic territory.

Socioeconomic status   A single, overall rank many sociologists use to describe people's positions in stratification systems.

Sociology   The systematic study of social systems and their effects on human experience and behavior.

Sociometry   The study of patterns of affection and loyalty that bind some group members more closely than others.

Spurious relationship   When two variables that have no causal connection are, nonetheless, statistically related to each other.

Status set   The entire collection of social statuses occupied by an individual.

Stereotype   A rigid, oversimplified belief that is applied to all members of a group or social category.

Surplus value   The value of goods and services that is kept by employers as profit after paying workers whatever is needed to sustain their labor power and reproduce themselves.

Symbolic interaction   The use of symbols by people to present themselves to others and interpret each other's behavior.

Technology   A society's accumulated knowledge of how to use the natural environment.

Temporary status   A situational or transitional status, usually occupied for a limited time.

Theoretical perspective   A non-explanatory, general framework that defines a point of view within a discipline, including basic assumptions that draw attention to particular aspects of a phenomenon and, therefore, generate particular kinds of questions about it.

Theory   A set of interrelated propositions designed to explain a phenomenon.

Time structure   The ways in which social relationships are defined, conditioned, and regulated by time.

Traditional authority   Authority that rests on the belief that the occupants of certain statuses are legitimately powerful because "that's that way it's always been."

Transitional status   A status occupied for a limited time as a "stepping stone" toward the occupancy of other statuses.

Value   An idea about what is socially desirable.

White-collar crime   Crimes that people are able to commit because of the power and opportunities afforded by social statuses—usually occupations—they occupy.

Worker   (See **Proletariat**.)

World economy (system)   The economic arrangement among all nations, in which there is a division of labor and no nation is self-sufficient.

World-system (dependency) theory   A theory that divides nations into three groups (based on the worldwide distribution of wealth and power) and argues that the economic development of societies depends on their position in the world system.

REFERENCES

— ◆ —

Allport, Gordon W. *The Nature of Prejudice:* Garden City, NY: Doubleday/Anchor, 1954.

Barnes, Barry. *About Science.* Oxford and New York: Basil Blackwell, 1985.

Berkman, Lisa F., and Syme, S. Leonard. "Social Networks, Host Resistance, and Mortality: A Nine-Year Follow-up Study of Alameda County Residents." *American Journal of Sociology*, 109,2 (1979): 186–203.

Bernard, Jessie. *The Future of Marriage.* New York: Bantam, 1972.

Blau, Peter M. *Exchange and Power in Social Life.* New York: Wiley, 1964.

Blumer, Herbert. *Symbolic Interactionism: Perspective and Method.* Englewood Cliffs, NJ: Prentice-Hall, 1969.

Bottomore, Tom, ed. *A Dictionary of Marxist Thought.* New York: Basil Blackwell, 1983.

Brown, Roger. *Social Psychology.* New York: The Free Press, 1965.

Brownmiller, Susan. *Against Our Will: Men, Women, and Rape.* New York: Simon and Schuster, 1975.

Cheng, Lucie, and Bonacich, Edna. *Labor Immigration under Capitalism: Asian Workers in the United States before World War II.* Berkeley: University of California Press, 1984.

Chirot, Daniel. *Social Change in the Modern Era.* San Diego: Harcourt Brace Jovanovich, 1986.

Cooley, Charles Horton. *Life and the Student.* New York: Knopf, 1927.

———. *Social Organization.* New York: Schocken Books, 1962. Originally published in 1909.

Cooper, Richard. "Rising Death Rates in the Soviet Union." *The New England Journal of Medicine* 304,21 (May 1981): 1259–65.

Coser, Lewis A. *Continuities in the Study of Social Conflict.* New York: The Free Press, 1967.

_____. *The Functions of Social Conflict*. Glencoe, IL: The Free Press, 1956.

Coser, Lewis A. ed. *The Idea of Social Structure: Papers in Honor of Robert K. Merton*. New York: Harcourt Brace Jovanovich, 1975.

Curtis, Helena. *Invitation to Biology*, 4th ed. New York: Worth, 1985.

Dahrendorf, Ralf. *Class and Class Conflict in Industrial Society*. Stanford, CA: Stanford University Press, 1959.

_____. "Toward a Theory of Social Conflict." *Journal of Conflict Resolution* 2 (June 1958): 170–83.

Davis, James A., and Smith, Tom W. *General Social Surveys, 1972–1990: Cumulative Codebook*. Chicago: National Opinion Research Center, 1990.

Democratic Staff of the Joint Economic Committee of the U.S. Congress. *The Concentration of Wealth in the United States*. Washington, D.C.: Joint Economic Committee, July 1986.

Demos, John. *A Little Commonwealth*. New York: Oxford, 1970.

_____. *Past, Present, and Personal: The Family and the Life Course in American History*. New York: Basic Books, 1986.

De Rougement, Denis. *Love in the Western World*. Montgomery Belgion, trans. Princeton, NJ: Princeton University Press, 1983.

Domhoff, G. William. *Who Rules America?*. Englewood Cliffs, NJ: Prentice-Hall, 1967.

Duncan, Otis Dudley, and Schnore, Leo F. "Cultural, Behavioral, and Ecological Perspectives in the Study of Social Organization." *American Journal of Sociology* 65 (1959).

Durkheim, Émile. *The Rules of the Sociological Method*. New York: The Free Press, 1964. Originally published in 1895.

_____. *Sociology and Philosophy*. New York: The Free Press, 1974. Originally published posthumously in 1924.

_____. *Suicide*. New York: The Free Press, 1951. Originally published in 1897.

Dutton, John. "Changes in Soviet Mortality Patterns, 1959–1977." *Population and Development Review* 5,2 (June 1979): 267–91.

Dworkin, Andrea. *Woman Hating*. New York: E. P. Dutton, 1974.

Edwards, Richard C., Reich, Michael, and Weisskopf, Thomas E., eds. *The Capitalist System: A Radical Analysis of American Society*. Englewood Cliffs, NJ: Prentice-Hall, 1986.

Ehrenreich, Barbara, and English, Deidre. *For Her Own Good: 150 Years of the Experts' Advice to Women*. Garden City, NY: Anchor, 1979.

Eisenstadt, S. N. *From Generation to Generation*. New York: The Free Press, 1956.

Eisler, Riane. *The Chalice and the Blade*. New York: Harper and Row, 1987.

Farley, Reynolds, and Allen, Walter R. *The Color Line and the Quality of Life in America*. New York: Russell Sage Foundation, 1987.

Fisher, Elizabeth. *Woman's Creation: Sexual Evolution and the Shaping of Society*. New York: McGraw-Hill, 1979.

Franks, David, and McCarthy, E. Doyle, eds. *The Sociology of Emotions*. JAI Press, 1988.

French, Marilyn. *Beyond Power*. New York: Summit, 1985.

Garfinkel, Harold. *Studies in Ethnomethodology*. Englewood Cliffs, NJ: Prentice-Hall, 1967.

Gartner, Rosemary. "The Victims of Homicide: A Temporal and Cross-National Comparison." *American Sociological Review*, 55,1 (1990): 92–106.

Gelles, Richard J. *The Violent Home*. Beverly Hills, CA; Sage, 1972.

Gelles, Richard J., and Cornell, C. P. *Intimate Violence in Families*. Beverly Hills, CA: Sage, 1985.

Gibson, James W. *The Perfect War: Technowar in Vietnam*. New York: Atlantic Monthly, 1989.

Giddens, Anthony. *The Constitution of Society: Outline of the Theory of Structuration*. Oxford: Polity Press, 1984.

Goffman, Erving. *Asylums*. New York: Anchor Books, 1961.

———. *Behavior in Public Places*. New York: The Free Press, 1963.

———. "Embarrassment and Social Organization." *American Journal of Sociology*, 62(1956–1957): 264–71.

———. *Encounters*. Indianapolis, IN: Bobbs-Merrill, 1961.

———. *Gender Advertisements*. New York: Harper Colophon, 1979.

———. *Interaction Ritual*. New York: Anchor Books, 1967.

———. *The Presentation of Self in Everyday Life*. New York: Doubleday, 1959.

———. *Stigma: Notes on the Management of a Spoiled Identity*. Englewood Cliffs, NJ: Prentice-Hall, 1963.

Gouldner, Alvin W. "The Norm of Reciprocity." *American Sociological Review* 25 (April 1960): 161–78.

Gove, Walter R. "Sex, Marital Status, and Mortality." *American Journal of Sociology* 79,1 (July 1973): 45–67.

Griffin, L. J. et al.. "Capitalism and Labor Organization." *American Sociological Review*, 51,2 (1986): 147–67.

Harrington, Michael. *The New American Poverty*. New York: Penguin, 1985.

Harris, Marvin. *Cannibals and Kings*. New York: Random House, 1977.

_____. *Cows, Pigs, Wars, and Witches*. New York: Random House, 1974.

_____. *Cultural Materialism*. New York: Random House, 1979.

Hawley, Amos H. *Human Ecology: A Theoretical Essay*. Chicago: University of Chicago Press, 1986.

Hollander, E. P. "Competence and Conformity in the Acceptance of Influence." *Journal of Abnormal and Social Psychology*, 51 (1960): 365–69.

Jacobs, D. "Inequality and Economic Crime." *Sociology and Social Research* 66,1 (1981): 12–28.

Jacobson, P. H. *American Marriage and Divorce*. New York: Rinehart, 1959.

Janis, I. L. *Air War and Emotional Stress*. New York: McGraw-Hill, 1951.

Johnson, Allan G. *Human Arrangements: An Introduction to Sociology*, 2nd ed. San Diego: Harcourt Brace Jovanovich, 1989.

Kammeyer, Kenneth, and Ginn, Helen. *An Introduction to Population*. Chicago: Dorsey Press, 1986.

Kennedy, Robert E., Jr. *The Irish: Emigration, Marriage, and Fertility*. Berkeley: University of California Press, 1973.

Kerbo, Harold R. *Social Stratification and Inequality: Class Conflict in the United States*. 2nd ed. New York: McGraw-Hill, 1991.

Langer, Susanne K. "The Growing Center of Knowledge." In *Philosophical Sketches*, pp. 145–46. Baltimore: Johns Hopkins Press, 1962.

Lasch, Christopher. *Haven in a Heartless World: The Family Besieged*. New York: Basic Books, 1977.

Lauer, R. H. *Temporal Man: The Meaning and Uses of Social Time.* New York: Praeger, 1981.

Lederer, Laura. *Take Back the Night: Women on Pornography.* New York: William Morrow, 1980.

Lee, Everett Lee. "A Theory of Migration." *Demography* 3 (1966): 47–59.

Lenski, Gerhard. *Power and Privilege.* New York: McGraw-Hill, 1966.

Lenski, Gerhard and Jean. *Human Societies,* 5th ed. New York: McGraw-Hill, 1987

Lester, David. *Why People Kill Themselves.* Springfield, IL: Charles C. Thomas, 1983.

Lyman, Stanford M., and Vidich, Arthur J. *Social Order and Public Philosophy: An Analysis and Interpretation of the Work of Herbert Blumer.* Fayetteville and London: University of Arkansas Press, 1988.

Malthus, Thomas. *Essay on the Principle of Population.* New York: Modern Library, 1960. Originally published in 1798.

Marx, Karl. *Capital: A Critical Analysis of Capitalist Production.* New York: International Publishers, 1967. Originally published in 1867.

Marx, Karl, and Engels, Freidrich. *The German Ideology.* New York: International Publishers, 1970. Originally published in 1846.

Massey, D. S. "Dimensions of the New Immigration to the United States and Prospects for Assimilation." *Annual Review of Sociology* 5 (1981): 57–85.

Massey, D. S. et al., *Return to Aztlan: The Social Process of International Migration from Western Mexico.* Berkeley: University of California Press, 1987.

Mead, George Herbert. *Mind, Self, and Society.* Chicago: University of Chicago Press, 1934.

Mead, Margaret. *Coming of Age in Samoa.* New York: Modern Library, 1953. Originally published in 1928.

Medea, A., and Thompson, K. *Against Rape.* New York: Farrar, Straus, and Giroux, 1974.

Mehan, Hugh, and Wood, Houston. *The Reality of Ethnomethodology.* New York: John Wiley and Sons, 1975.

Meltzer, Bernard N., and Petras, Jerome W. "The Chicago and Iowa Schools of Symbolic Interactionism," in T. Shibutani, ed.,

Human Nature and Collective Behavior. Englewood Cliffs, NJ: Prentice-Hall, 1970.

Merton, Robert K. "Discrimination and the American Creed." In *Sociological Ambivalence.* New York: The Free Press, 1976.

_____. "Our Sociological Vernacular." *Columbia* (November 1981): 42–44.

_____. *Social Theory and Social Structure,* enl. ed. New York: The Free Press, 1968.

_____. "The Sociology of Social Problems." In Robert K. Merton and Robert Nisbet, eds., *Contemporary Social Problems,* 4th ed. New York: Harcourt Brace Jovanovich, 1976.

Miller, N., and Brewer, M. B., eds. *Groups in Contact: The Psychology of Desegregation.* New York: Academic Press, 1984.

Mills, C. Wright. *The Sociological Imagination.* New York: Oxford University Press, 1959.

Mintz, B. "The President's Cabinet, 1897–1972: A Contribution to the Power Structure Debate." *Insurgent Sociologist* 5(1975): 131–48.

Moreno, J. L. "Sociometry and the Cultural Order." *Sociometry* 6 (1943): 299–344.

Moskos, Charles C. "Why Men Fight: American Combat Soldiers in Vietnam." *Transaction,* 7(1) (1969).

Murray, Charles. *Losing Ground.* New York: Basic Books, 1984.

Myrdal, Gunnar. *An American Dilemma.* New York: Harper and Row, 1945.

Namboodiri, Krishnan. "Ecological Demography: Its Place in Sociology." *American Sociological Review,* 53,4 (1990): 619–33.

National Center for Health Statistics. *Vital Statistics of the United States.* Washington, D.C.: U.S. Government Printing office.

Neustadt, R. E., and May, E. R. *Thinking in Time.* New York: The Free Press, 1986.

O'Gorman, Hubert J. "The Discovery of Pluralistic Ignorance." *Journal of the History of the Behavioral Sciences,* 22 (October 1986): 333–47.

_____. "White and Black Perceptions of Racial Values." *Public Opinion Quarterly* 43(1979): 48–59.

Painter, N. I. *Standing at Armageddon: The United States, 1877–1919.* New York: W. W. Norton and Company, 1987.

Parenti, Michael. *Inventing Reality*. New York: St. Martin's Press, 1985.

Parsons, Talcott. *The Social System*. New York: The Free Press, 1951.

Perrow, Charles. *Normal Accidents*. New York: Basic Books, 1984.

Petersen, William. "A General Typology of Migration." *American Sociological Review*, 23 (1958): 256–65.

Piven, Frances Fox, and Cloward, Richard A. *Why Americans Don't Vote*. New York: Pantheon, 1988.

Preston, Samuel. "An International Comparison of Excessive Adult Mortality." *Population Studies* 24 (1970): 5–20.

Ravenstein, E. G. "The Laws of Migration." *Journal of the Royal Statistical Society* 48, Part II (1885): 61–235.

_____. "The Laws of Migration." *Journal of the Royal Statistical Society* 52 (1889): 241–305.

Ridgeway, C. L. "Nonconformity, Competence, and Influence in Groups." *American Sociological Review*, 46 (June 1981): 333–47.

Robinson, W. P. *Language and Social Behavior*. Baltimore, MD: Penguin, 1972.

Rosen, Sherwin, and Taubman, Paul. "Changes in the Impact of Education and Income on Mortality in the U.S." In Linda DelBene and Foritz Schueren, eds., *Statistical Uses of Administrative Records with Emphasis on Mortality and Disability Research*. Washington, D.C.: Department of Health, Education and Welfare, Social Security Administration, Office of Research Statistics, 1979.

Rosenthal, Phil. "In Spite of What Executives Say, Proposed Media Conglomerate Is Development to Be Feared." The Hartford *Courant*, April 2, 1989, p. G1. Originally published in the Los Angeles *Daily News*.

Russell, Diana E. H. *Rape in Marriage*. New York: Macmillan, 1982.

_____. *The Secret Trauma: Incest in the Lives of Girls and Women*. New York: Basic Books, 1986.

_____. *Sexual Exploitation: Rape, Child Sexual Abuse, and Workplace Harassment*. Beverly Hills, CA: Sage, 1984.

Schur, Edwin. *Labeling Women Deviant: Gender, Stigma, and Social Control*. New York: Random House, 1984.

Shils, Edward. A., and Janowitz, Morris. "Cohesion and Disintegration in the Wehrmacht in World War II." *Public Opinion Quarterly*, 12 (Summer 1948): 280–315.

Shupe, A. et al. *Violent Men, Violent Couples: The Dynamics of Domestic Violence*. Lexington, MA: Lexington Books, 1987.

Skinner, B. F. *Beyond Freedom and Dignity*. New York: Knopf, 1971.

Smith, Joan. *Social Issues and the Social Order: The Contradictions of Capitalism*. Boston: Little Brown, 1981.

Sommer, Robert. *Personal Space: The Behavioral Analysis of Design*. Englewood Cliffs, NJ: Prentice-Hall, 1969.

South, S. J. "Economic Conditions and the Divorce Rate." *Journal of Marriage and the Family*, 47,1 (1985): 31–41.

Straus, Murray et al. *Behind Closed Doors*. New York: Anchor, 1980.

Thomas, W. I. and Dorothy S. *The Child in America*. New York: Knopf, 1928.

Tuchman, Barbara. *The March of Folly: From Troy to Vietnam*. New York: Knopf, 1984.

U.S. Census Bureau. *Statistical Abstract of the United States, 1987*. Washington, D.C.: U.S. Government Printing Office, 1986.

U.S. Department of Commerce. *Historical Statistics of the United States, Colonial Times to 1970*. Washington, D.C.: U.S. Government Printing Office, 1975, Parts 1 and 2.

U.S. Department of Justice. "Criminal Victimization in the United States: 1985." Washington, D.C.: U.S. Government Printing Office, 1987.

Van Creveld, M. *Fighting Power: German and U.S. Army Performance, 1939–1945*. Westport, CT: Greenwood Press, 1981.

Vanneman, R., and Cannon, L. W. *The American Perception of Class*. Philadelphia: Temple University Press, 1987.

Wallerstein, Immanual. *The Capitalist World Economy*. Cambridge: Cambridge University Press, 1979.

_____. *The Modern World System*. New York: Academic Press, 1976.

_____. *The Modern World System II: Mercantilism and the Consolidation of the European World Economy, 1600–1750*. New York: Academic Press, 1980.

Weber, Max. *The Theory of Social and Economic Organization*. New York: Oxford University Press, 1947. Originally published posthumously in 1925.

Weitzman, Lenore. *The Divorce Revolution: The Unexpected Social and Economic Consequences of Divorce on Women and Children in America.* New York: The Free Press, 1985.

Whelpton, Pascal, and Kaiser, Clyde V. "Social and Psychological Factors Affecting Fertility." *Milbank Memorial Fund Quarterly*, 2 (1950).

World Bank. *World Development Report 1983.* New York: Oxford University Press, 1983.

Wrong, Dennis. *Power: Its Forms, Bases, and Uses.* New York: Harper and Row, 1980.

Zelizer, Viviana. *Pricing the Priceless Child: The Changing Social Value of Children.* New York: Basic Books, 1985.

Zerubavel, E. *The Seven Day Circle: The History and Meaning of the Week.* New York: The Free Press/Macmillan, 1985.

INDEX

——— ◆ ———

D E F G H I J
2 3 4 5 6 7 8 9